OCT 1 8 2018

NO LONGER PROPERTY OF
SEATTLE PUBLIC LIBRARY

D0583466

THE **LITTLE BOOK** OF **ROCK** AND **ROLL** Wisdom

THE **LITTLE BOOK** OF **ROCK** AND **ROLL** *Wisdom*

MIKE KATZ AND CRISPIN KOTT

ILLUSTRATIONS BY JASON MALMBERG

GUILFORD, CONNECTICUT

An imprint of The Rowman & Littlefield Publishing Group, Inc.
4501 Forbes Blvd., Ste. 200
Lanham, MD 20706
www.rowman.com

Distributed by NATIONAL BOOK NETWORK

Copyright © 2018 Mike Katz and Crispin Kott

Illustrations © 2018 Rowman & Littlefield Publishing Group, Inc.

All rights reserved. No part of this book may be reproduced in any form or by any electronic or mechanical means, including information storage and retrieval systems, without written permission from the publisher, except by a reviewer who may quote passages in a review.

British Library Cataloguing in Publication Information available

Library of Congress Cataloging-in-Publication Data
Names: Katz, Mike, 1962- author. | Kott, Crispin, author. | Malmberg, Jason, illustrator.
Title: The little book of rock and roll wisdom / Mike Katz and Crispin Kott;
illustrations by Jason Malmberg.
Description: Guilford, Connecticut : Lyons Press, 2018.
Identifiers: LCCN 2018017589 | ISBN 9781493035618 (hardcover)
ISBN 9781493035625 (e-book)
Subjects: LCSH: Rock music--Miscellanea. | Rock musicians--Quotations,
maxims, etc. | Rock music--Humor.
Classification: LCC ML3534 .K38 2018 | DDC 781.66--dc23 LC record available at
https://lccn.loc.gov/2018017589

™

The paper used in this publication meets the minimum requirements of American National Standard for Information Sciences—Permanence of Paper for Printed Library Materials, ANSI/NISO Z39.48-1992.

Printed in the United States of America

contents

chapter one
REBELLION, REVOLUTION, *and* *Deep Thinking*

Rock & Roll has a long association with the idea of rebellion, offending at various times parents, squares, older generations, and, perhaps most famously, "the man." But while rebellion and revolution are through

lines in Rock & Roll, rock stars rarely agree on how to fight the power, who the power even is, or where to draw inspiration from as they fight the good fight…whatever that is.

The Rock & Roll Wisdom Playlist

The Beatles—"Revolution"
The Clash—"Know Your Rights"
Jarvis Cocker—"Running the World"
The Rolling Stones—"Street Fighting Man"
The Special A.K.A.—"Racist Friend"

FRANK ZAPPA

"PEOPLE ARE STUPID. THEY NEVER STOP TO QUESTION THINGS. THEY JUST ACCEPT. CAN YOU IMAGINE A NATION WHO NEVER QUESTIONS THE VALIDITY OF CHEERLEADERS AND POM-POMS?"

Rolling Stone, October 12, 1968

REBELLION, REVOLUTION, AND DEEP THINKING

MICK JAGGER
THE ROLLING STONES

"THE ONLY HANG UP IS THE FUZZ. NOW THAT'S A DRAG. ONCE YOU GET IN TROUBLE WITH THE POLICE, YOU'RE ALWAYS IN TROUBLE AND THAT'S IT. BEFORE, WE WERE NEVER IN TROUBLE AND THEY WERE ALWAYS VERY NICE TO US. THEY SHOULD BE LOOKING AFTER PEOPLE AND TURNING AMERICAN TOURISTS AWAY FROM PICCADILLY CIRCUS."

Rolling Stone, October 12, 1968

"I AIN'T GONNA BE ANY CELLOPHANE SOCIAL-ITE. THEY DON'T GET ME IN ANY CELLOPHANE CAGE. NOBODY CAGES ME."

JIMI HENDRIX

Hit Parader, November 1969

REBELLION, REVOLUTION, AND DEEP THINKING

"I THINK EVERYBODY WHO HAS A BRAIN SHOULD GET INVOLVED IN POLITICS. WORKING WITHIN. NOT CRITICIZING IT FROM THE OUTSIDE. BECOME AN ACTIVE PARTICIPANT, NO MATTER HOW FEEBLE YOU THINK THE EFFORT IS."

CASS ELLIOTT
THE MAMAS AND THE PAPAS

Rolling Stone, October 26, 1968

Pitchfork, March 16, 2017

"I DON'T BELIEVE IN FUCKING SHIT UP FROM THE INSIDE. THAT MEANS YOU HAVE ENOUGH FAITH IN THE SYSTEM THAT IT CAN BE PERFECTED IN SOME WAY. I DON'T BELIEVE IN THAT SYSTEM, SO I DON'T HAVE ANY PETU-LANT DESIRE TO TOY WITH OR ANTAGONIZE IT."

FATHER JOHN MISTY

REBELLION, REVOLUTION, AND DEEP THINKING

Creem, September 1975

"ESSENTIALLY, CITY ADMINISTRATIONS DON'T LIKE ROCK &
ROLL. AND THEY DON'T LIKE ROCK & ROLL IN THEIR PARKS.
AND THEY DON'T LIKE PEOPLE CONGREGATING IN GROUPS OF
MORE THAN THREE. THE WHOLE THING SCARES 'EM. THEY'RE
SCARED OF EIGHT MILLION PEOPLE AND ANOTHER ALTAMONT.
THAT'S A CONVENIENT EXCUSE NOW. THEY START OFF SAYING
'NO, YOU CAN'T DO ONE' AND YOU WORK IT FROM THERE."

PAUL KANTNER
JEFFERSON STARSHIP

JIM MORRISON
THE DOORS

"I THINK YOUR POLITICS, YOUR RELIGION, YOUR PHILOSOPHY ARE NOT SO MUCH WHAT YOU SMOKE, WHAT YOU DRINK, WHAT YOU WEAR ... YOUR HAIR, YOUR FACE, WHAT YOU'VE DONE. YOUR RELIGION OR YOUR POLITICS IS WHAT YOU DEVOTE THE MAJORITY OF YOUR TIME TO. NOTHING MORE, NOTHING LESS."

Rolling Stone, July 26, 1969

REBELLION, REVOLUTION, AND DEEP THINKING

14

PAUL SIMON

"ALL THE MAIL THAT CAME INTO US WAS SCREAMING AT US: JUST SING—WE LOVE THE WAY YOU SING BUT WE'RE NOT INTERESTED IN YOUR POLITICAL OPINION OR YOUR VIEW OF SOCIETY—JUST SING. I USED TO SAY TO ARTIE IT'S LIKE IF YOU DECIDED TO GO TO THE BATHROOM AND SOMEBODY SAID, 'DON'T GO TO THE BATHROOM. JUST SING, THAT'S WHAT YOU DO. DON'T DO ANYTHING ELSE. DON'T MAKE BACON IN THE MORNING. YOU'RE NOT A BACON MAKER, YOU SING.'"

Rolling Stone, May 28, 1970

"I'VE NEVER SEEN ANYTHING SOLVED BY VIOLENCE. HISTORY USUALLY COMES BACK TO WHERE IT ALL BEGAN; YOU EITHER LEARN TO ASSIMILATE OR EXTERMINATE, AND NOT JUST YOUR ENEMY, BUT YOURSELF."

JOHN LYDON

Rotten: No Irish, No Blacks, No Dogs,
St. Martin's Press, 1993

REBELLION, REVOLUTION, AND DEEP THINKING

"I REALLY DON'T LIKE VIOLENCE. I HATE FIGHTS, I AVOID THEM. IT JUST SEEMS SO STUPID IT REPELS ME. I UNDERSTAND BREAKING GUITARS ONSTAGE, I EVEN KICKED AN AMP TO DEATH MYSELF ONE NIGHT, BUT I DON'T GET ANY THRILL OUT OF WITNESSING DESTRUCTION. I'D RATHER SEE A GUY DO IT AS A JOKE THAN DO IT BECAUSE OF AN INABILITY TO CONTROL HIS TEMPER. A FRIEND OF MINE AND I TORE A TYPEWRITER TO BITS ONE NIGHT, BUT IT WAS OUT OF FUN. LIKE, 'WANNA SEE A KEY?' ..RIP!"

TOM VERLAINE
TELEVISION

Creem, May 1977

Melody Maker, December 13, 1980

"I'M IN GANDHI'S ARMY AND LUTHER KING'S ARMY. I TRIED FIGHTING VIOLENCE WITH VIOLENCE. I TRIED IT IN HAMBURG AND I NEARLY MURDERED SOME GUY, BECAUSE I WAS OUT OF ORDER. THEY WERE OUT OF ORDER, BUT THAT'S NO EXCUSE FOR ME TO GET OUT OF ORDER, AND I ONLY JUST GOT OUT OF JAIL ALIVE. SO FROM THAT DAY ON, LIFE WAS TEACHING ME SOME-THING AND LUTHER KING AND GANDHI WERE RIGHT, YOU CAN'T FIGHT VIOLENCE WITH VIOLENCE."

JOE STRUMMER
THE CLASH

REBELLION, REVOLUTION, AND DEEP THINKING

NME, December 22, 1984

"I'M NOT TOTALLY AVERSE TO VIOLENCE. I THINK IT'S QUITE ATTRACTIVELY NECESSARY IN SOME EXTREMES."

MORRISSEY
THE SMITHS

PAUL SIMONON
THE CLASH

"THE ENGLISH PEOPLE ARE PRETTY STRANGE IN SOME WAYS. I READ THERE WAS A TIME AROUND 1900 WHEN EVERYBODY WAS GOING TO STRIKE AND MEET ON HYDE PARK CORNER AND HAVE A REVOLUTION. BUT IT RAINED THAT DAY, SO NOBODY SHOWED UP."

Creem, May 1979

REBELLION, REVOLUTION, AND DEEP THINKING

GARY VALENTINE
BLONDIE

"COMIC BOOKS ARE GONNA SHAPE THE NEXT GENERATION. THEY'RE GONNA READ COMIC BOOKS AND BE FOR LAW AND ORDER AND WEAR MASKS."

Creem, May 1977

"SOMETIMES IT'S HARD FOR ME TO SEE WHAT'S GOING ON, COS I NEVER SURROUND MYSELF WITH ANYONE WHO HAS THE SLIGHTEST INKLING OF RACISM. IT MAKES ME SO SICK, I JUST WANNA SHIT ON THEIR FACES. THERE'S DEFINITELY A MONSTROUS RACISM PROBLEM. THAT'S ONE OF THE MAIN THINGS WE STAND AGAINST, IF WE STAND AGAINST ANYTHING."

FLEA
RED HOT CHILI PEPPERS

NME, September 28, 1985

REBELLION, REVOLUTION, AND DEEP THINKING

"I'M A CELEBRITY AND I DON'T HAVE TO WAIT FOR CABS, I DON'T HAVE TO BOOK RESTAURANTS AND NOBODY TREATS ME LIKE SOMEBODY OFF THE STREET. THEREFORE IT'D BE THE EASIEST THING IMAGINABLE FOR ME TO SAY THAT, YES, THERE IS NO MORE OPPRESSION AND DISCRIMINATION AND I'VE WON THIS BATTLE AND THAT BATTLE, BUT I HAVE TO KEEP HOLD OF THE FACT THAT THAT'S JUST NOT TRUE."

BOY GEORGE
CULTURE CLUB

NME, September 29, 1984

Uncut, July 2005

"SEE, THERE WAS A POINT IN THE '60S OR '70S WHEN IT ALL BECAME ABOUT ICONS. PEOPLE WOULD SIT AROUND DEBATING WHAT THE NEXT BEATLES ALBUM WAS GOING TO SAY—LIKE THE BEATLES WERE GOING TO TELL US WHERE IT'S AT. AS IF THE BEATLES WERE A RELIGION OR BOB DYLAN WAS THE MAN WHO HAD THE WORD—EVEN THOUGH HE REJECTED ALL THAT SHIT. WELL, I REJECT IT, TOO. I ALWAYS HAVE DONE. BUT IT'S STILL THE SAME. AFTER ALL THIS TIME, IT'S STILL BEING PERPETUATED."

VAN MORRISON

REBELLION, REVOLUTION, AND DEEP THINKING

NME, February 23, 1985

"I WAS DRIVING DOWN THE SAN DIEGO FREEWAY AND GOT PASSED BY A $21,000 CADILLAC SEVILLE, THE STATUS SYMBOL OF THE RIGHT-WING UPPER-MIDDLE-CLASS AMERICAN BOURGEOISIE—ALL THE GUYS WITH THE BLUE BLAZERS WITH THE CRESTS AND THE GREY PANTS—AND THERE WAS THIS GRATEFUL DEAD 'DEADHEAD' BUMPER STICKER ON IT!"

DON HENLEY

PATTI SMITH

"I WAKE UP EVERY DAY AND I'M HALF APACHE. IT'S LIKE I HAVE NOWHERE TO PUT MY TOMAHAWK, SO I HAVE TO SCALP WITH MY ELECTRIC GUITAR. MY GUITAR IS MY INSTRUMENT OF BATTLE. THAT'S WHY I LIKE ROCK & ROLL—IT GIVES A LITTLE 100-POUND MONKEY A CHANCE TO BE A SOLDIER. IT'S THE ONLY MACHINE GUN I EVER GOT TO HOLD. I CAN'T HELP IT, WE WERE BORN OUT OF VIOLENT TIMES. I'M A WAR BABY, I WAS BORN OUT OF WAR AND NEVER GOT A CHANCE TO BE A SOLDIER MYSELF, EXCEPT NOW IN ROCK & ROLL, AND MY FIGHT IS TO KEEP ROCK & ROLL ALIVE AND TO CONTINUE ROCK & ROLL, NOW MORE THAN EVER."

ZigZag, June, 1978

REBELLION, REVOLUTION, AND DEEP THINKING

RICK WAKEMAN

"I THINK EVERY PERFORMER IS A JEKYLL AND HYDE. WHEN YOU ARE PLAYING, IT'S LIKE GOING INTO A TRANCE, NOT LIKE MEDITATION OR ANYTHING. BUT SOMEHOW YOUR WHOLE MIND IS GEARED TO ONE THING—THE MUSIC— AND EVERYTHING ELSE IS BLOTTED OUT."

Creem, February 1975

"I THINK MUSIC IS MAGIC, I THINK IT'S ALWAYS BEEN MANKIND'S PARTY. BUT I THINK WHAT HAPPENS IS THERE ARE PERIPHERAL THINGS, CHICKS, GLORY, MONEY, FAME. 'I MUST BE SMART, LOOK HOW MANY PEOPLE ARE LISTENING'. I THINK ALL THOSE THINGS PULL YOU AWAY FROM THE CENTRAL ISSUE OF MUSIC AND ARE DESTRUCTIVE TO IT."

DAVID CROSBY

The Guardian, March 3, 1989

REBELLION, REVOLUTION, AND DEEP THINKING

"I BELIEVE WE ARE MOVING TOWARD A NEW AGE IN IDEAS AND EVENTS. ASTROLOGICALLY WE ARE AT THE END OF THE AGE CALLED THE PISCES AGE—AT THE BEGINNING OF WHICH PEOPLE LIKE CHRIST WERE BORN. WE ARE SOON TO BEGIN THE AGE OF AQUARIUS, IN WHICH EVENTS AS IMPORTANT AS THOSE AT THE BEGINNING OF PISCES ARE LIKELY TO OCCUR. THERE IS A YOUNG REVOLUTION IN THOUGHT AND MANNER ABOUT TO TAKE PLACE."

BRIAN JONES
THE ROLLING STONES

NME, February 4, 1967

Induction of Lou Reed to the Rock & Roll Hall of Fame, April 18, 2015

"I'M REMINDED ALSO OF THE THREE RULES WE CAME UP WITH, RULES TO LIVE BY. AND I'M JUST GOING TO TELL YOU WHAT THEY ARE BECAUSE THEY COME IN REALLY HANDY. BECAUSE THINGS HAPPEN SO FAST, IT'S ALWAYS GOOD TO HAVE A FEW, LIKE, WATCHWORDS TO FALL BACK ON. AND THE FIRST ONE IS: ONE. DON'T BE AFRAID OF ANYONE. NOW, CAN YOU IMAGINE LIVING YOUR LIFE AFRAID OF NO ONE? TWO. GET A REALLY GOOD BULLSHIT DETECTOR. AND THREE. THREE IS BE REALLY, REALLY TENDER. AND WITH THOSE THREE THINGS, YOU DON'T NEED ANYTHING ELSE."

LAURIE ANDERSON

REBELLION, REVOLUTION, AND DEEP THINKING

Rotten: No Irish, No Blacks, No Dogs,
St. Martin's Press, 1993

"CHAOS WAS MY PHILOSOPHY. OH YEAH. HAVE NO RULES. IF PEOPLE START TO BUILD FENCES AROUND YOU, BREAK OUT AND DO SOMETHING ELSE. YOU SHOULD NEVER, EVER BE UNDER-STOOD COMPLETELY. THAT'S LIKE THE KISS OF DEATH, ISN'T IT?"

JOHN LYDON

JOE STRUMMER
THE CLASH

"THERE'S TOO MANY RULES BECAUSE RULE ONE IS, THERE IS NO RULE AND THAT WAS THE FIRST RULE OF PUNK AND THE LAST. THAT KIND OF ATTITUDE, WE CAN DO WHAT WE WANT TO DO."

Melody Maker, December 13, 1980

REBELLION, REVOLUTION, AND DEEP THINKING

LEONARD
COHEN

"I WISH THE WOMEN WOULD HURRY UP AND TAKE OVER. IT'S GOING TO HAPPEN SO LET'S GET IT OVER WITH. THEN WE CAN FINALLY RECOGNIZE THAT WOMEN REALLY ARE THE MINDS AND THE FORCE THAT HOLDS EVERYTHING TOGETHER; AND MEN REALLY ARE GOS-SIPS AND ARTISTS. THEN WE COULD GET ABOUT OUR CHILDISH WORK AND THEY COULD KEEP THE WORLD GOING. I REALLY AM FOR THE MATRIARCHY."

New York Times, January 28, 1968

"I'D RULE THIS WORLD SO WELL. I'D BE SO FUCKING FAIR. I'D BE THE BEST OMNIPOTENT BEING EVER."

COURTNEY LOVE
HOLE

Melody Maker, February 19, 1994

REBELLION, REVOLUTION, AND DEEP THINKING

"I KEEP SAYING TO MY FRIENDS, 'WHERE ARE THE FUCKING AGITATORS? WHERE ARE THE YOUNG PEOPLE IN COMPLETE DISSENT WITH THE MAINSTREAM?' I DON'T SEE IT. I FEEL LIKE THEY HAVE BEEN ANESTHETIZED BY TWITTER AND FACEBOOK AND WHAT I CALL THE 'LIKE' CULTURE. YOUNG PEOPLE MEASURE HOW POPULAR THEY ARE BY HOW MANY LIKES THEY HAVE ON FACEBOOK AND HOW MANY PEOPLE ARE FOLLOWING THEM ON TWITTER. THERE'S THIS WHOLE CULTURE OBSESSED WITH BEING LIKED! OF COURSE THERE CAN'T BE ANY DISSENT WHEN YOU'RE OBSESSED WITH BEING LIKED AND LOVED AND WORSHIPPED."

SHIRLEY MANSON
GARBAGE

The Talks, *New York Times*,
June 12, 2013

Select, April 1994

"I DON'T THINK OF SOME GUY SITTING ON A CLOUD, BUT I KNOW THAT THERE HAD TO BE PRIME MOVER TO SET EVERYTHING IN MOTION. I BELIEVE IN A GREATER FORCE, A SUPREME BEING AROUND US. IN FACT, I RECENTLY HAD AN ARGUMENT ON THIS SUBJECT WITH SOME VEHEMENT ATHEISTS. I MEAN, USUALLY I CAN DEAL WITH AGNOS-TICS AND ATHEISTS, BUT NOT VEHEMENT ONES."

STEPHEN MALKMUS
PAVEMENT

REBELLION, REVOLUTION, AND DEEP THINKING

Rolling Stone, May 14, 1970

"I BELIEVE ROCK CAN DO ANYTHING, IT'S THE ULTIMATE VEHICLE FOR EVERYTHING. IT'S THE ULTIMATE VEHICLE FOR SAYING ANYTHING, FOR PUTTING DOWN ANYTHING, FOR BUILDING UP ANYTHING, FOR KILLING AND CREATING."

PETE TOWNSHEND
THE WHO

FIVE ROCK & ROLL STARS
WHO'VE FOUGHT THE LAW
and the law Won

1. CHUCK BERRY—Rock & Roll pioneer Chuck Berry had numerous brushes with the law, with his arrest two days before Christmas in 1959 eventually leading to nearly two years in a federal prison on a charge of violating the Mann Act. Berry later served four months in prison for tax evasion.

2. PAUL SIMONON—Former Clash bass guitarist Paul Simonon was arrested in June 2011 after occupying the Leiv Eriksson oil rig off the coast of Greenland. Simonon and 17 other activists were protesting Arctic oil drilling for Greenpeace. Simonon had previously been arrested with Clash drummer Topper Headon for shooting pigeons from a London rooftop.

3. DAVID CROSBY—Former Byrd David Crosby's 1982 arrest on drugs and weapons charges yielded a nine-month stint in a Texas state prison. Croz also ran afoul of the law in 1985 and 2004, with drugs and weapons a factor both times.

4. PAUL MCCARTNEY—A few years after the 1970 breakup of the Beatles, Paul McCartney was fined in both Sweden and

Scotland for charges relating to marijuana. But it wasn't until early 1980 when Japanese customs officials found cannabis in his luggage that he actually went to jail. Macca spent 10 days in a local jail before Japanese authorities released and deported him. He was arrested for possession once more, while on holiday in Barbados in 1984, but he paid a fine and was not locked up. In 2015, McCartney revealed that he'd given up smoking marijuana to set an example for his kids and grandkids.

5. SID VICIOUS—In October 1978, former Sex Pistols bass player John "Sid Vicious" Ritchie was arrested and charged with murder in the stabbing death of his girlfriend Nancy Spungen at the Hotel Chelsea in New York City. He was released on bail and awaiting pre-trial when he was arrested for assault that December after attacking Todd Smith, singer Patti Smith's brother, at Hurrah, a Manhattan punk club. Vicious spent 55 days detoxing from a heroin addiction in jail at Rikers Island before his release on bail on February 1, 1979. He died of an overdose early the next morning.

chapter two
LOVE AND
Sex

Rock & Roll has, since its inception, demonstrated an equal capacity for both romantic tenderness and insatiable carnality. A unique irreverence toward both is what has kept it fun and amusing.

The Rock & Roll Wisdom Playlist

The Beach Boys—"God Only Knows"
J. Geils Band—"Love Stinks"
Liz Phair—"Supernova"
Nine Inch Nails—"Closer"
The Beatles—"Something"

PRINCE

"SEX IS SOMETHING WE CAN ALL UNDERSTAND. IT'S LIMITLESS."

Los Angeles Times, November 21, 1982

LOVE AND SEX

DAVID CROSBY

"THE PROBLEM IS THAT I'VE EXPLORED ABOUT EVERY AVENUE OF SEX THAT I'VE HEARD OF, OK? THE TROUBLE IS THAT I LIKE 'EM, MOST OF 'EM. I'M NOT TOO FOND OF THE BATHROOM TRIPS, BUT ASIDE FROM THAT IN THE CATALOG OF SEXUAL HISTORY I THINK THAT THERE ARE VERY FEW THINGS THAT I DON'T LIKE. WHICH MAKES ME, BY MOST PEOPLE'S STANDARDS, A FREAK."

Rolling Stone, July 23, 1970

"WELL, CAN I SAY FIRST THERE'S NO SUCH THING AS BISEXUALITY, NO SUCH FUCKING THING. YOU DEFINITELY HAVE A PREFERENCE—EVERYONE HAS A PREFERENCE. I'VE HAD A LOT OF SEX, A LOT, AND I'VE FUCKED, I DUNNO, FOURTEEN GIRLS? FIFTEEN? BUT WHEN IT COMES DOWN TO IT, I JUST WANT SOMEONE TO STICK IT IN, Y'KNOW?"

COURTNEY LOVE
HOLE

Melody Maker, February 19, 1994

LOVE AND SEX

"...ON MORE THAN ONE OCCASION WE USED TONY [IOMMI] AS A HONEY TRAP—'COS HE WAS THE ONE ALL THE CHICKS WANTED TO BANG. WHAT WOULD HAPPEN IS, HE'D GO UPSTAIRS TO OUR ROOM AND START FUMBLING AROUND WITH SOME GROUPIE ON ONE OF THE BUNKS, AND I'D CRAWL OVER ON MY ELBOWS—COMMANDO-STYLE—TO WHERE SHE'D LEFT HER HANDBAG, AND SWIPE WHATEVER DOUGH I COULD FIND. I AIN'T PROUD OF IT, BUT WE HAD TO FUCKING EAT SOMEHOW."

OZZY OSBOURNE

I Am Ozzy,
Grand Central Publishing, 2010

Faithfull: An Autobiography,
Cooper Square Press, 1994

"I'VE SPENT MOST OF MY LIFE TRYING TO GRASP THAT PARTICULAR BIT OF SEXUAL ETIQUETTE AND, LET'S FACE IT, I STILL DON'T GET IT. WHEN YOU'RE NASTY THEY PURSUE YOU LIKE CRAZY AND WHEN YOU'RE NICE THEY RUN AWAY SCREAMING. THOSE COURTLY GAMES ARE SOMETHING I'VE NEVER BEEN VERY GOOD AT."

MARIANNE FAITHFULL

LOVE AND SEX

Creem, October 1979

"IN THE FRENCH ADVERTISEMENTS FOR BRAS THEY SAY, 'HIDE IT SUBTLY 'CAUSE A MAN DOESN'T LIKE TO DISCOVER SOMETHING ON THE OUTSIDE.' IT'S SEXIER NOT TO REVEAL EVERYTHING, TO ADD A DEGREE OF DISCOVERY."

TINA WEYMOUTH
TALKING HEADS

KIM GORDON
SONIC YOUTH

"AROUND THAT TIME I ALSO REMEMBER [MY MOTHER] TELLING ME THAT BOYS MIGHT LIKE GIRLS BECAUSE OF THE WAY THEY LOOKED, BUT THE QUALITY OF A GIRL'S BRAIN WAS THE TICKET TO A MORE SATISFYING RELATIONSHIP. IT WAS ADVICE THAT CAUSED ME ALL KINDS OF NEUROSES. IT ALSO PROVED TO BE WRONG."

Girl in a Band: A Memoir,
Dey Street Books, 2015

LOVE AND SEX

CHRISSIE HYNDE
THE PRETENDERS

"SO-CALLED WOMEN'S LIB WAS RATHER MISLED BY THE PILL. WOMEN WEREN'T IN CONTROL OF THEIR BODIES; THE DRUG WAS. TAKING PROCREATION OUT OF THE EQUATION WAS TURNING WOMEN INTO SEX TOYS. NO ONE SEEMED TO MIND.
I KNOW I DIDN'T."

Reckless: My Life as a Pretender,
Doubleday, 2015

"YOU COME OUT OF SCHOOL, YOU KNOW, AND YOU GET INTO A GROUP AND YOU'VE GOT THOUSANDS OF CHICKS THERE. I MEAN YOU WERE AT SCHOOL AND YOU WERE PIMPLY AND NO ONE WANTED TO KNOW YOU. AND THEN THERE YOU ARE ON STAGE WITH THOUSANDS OF LITTLE GIRLS SCREAMING THEIR HEAD OFF. MAN, IT'S POWER! ... WHEW!"

ERIC CLAPTON
CREAM

Rolling Stone, May 11, 1968

LOVE AND SEX

"AND YOU HAVE TO REMEMBER, I WAS AN UGLY SON OF A BITCH. AT MY BEST, I LOOKED LIKE A DOG AT BIRTH. BUT, NOW THAT I WAS IN THIS FAMOUS BAND, I WAS IN A POSITION WHERE I COULD MOUNT ANYBODY'S GIRLFRIEND AND MOTHER, OFTEN AT THE SAME TIME. THAT'S THE MAGIC OF ROCK & ROLL RIGHT THERE. IT MEANS THAT EVEN MEAT LOAF CAN GET SOME PUSS."

GENE SIMMONS
KISS

Uncut, March 2006

"I HATE MEN WHO CAN ONLY SEE WOMEN IN A SEXUAL WAY—TO ME THAT'S CRIMINAL AND I WANT TO CHANGE THAT. I DON'T RECOGNIZE SUCH TERMS AS HETEROSEXUAL, HOMOSEXUAL, BISEXUAL, AND I THINK IT'S IMPORTANT THAT THERE'S SOMEONE IN POP MUSIC WHO'S LIKE THAT. THESE WORDS DO GREAT DAMAGE, THEY CONFUSE PEOPLE AND THEY MAKE PEOPLE UNHAPPY SO I WANT TO DO AWAY WITH THEM,"

MORRISSEY THE SMITHS

LOVE AND SEX

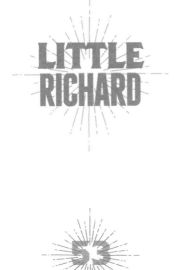

NME, March 23, 1985

"I HAVE GAY FRIENDS ALL OVER THE WORLD, BISEXUAL FRIENDS, STRAIGHT FRIENDS, LESBIANS, AND THEY HAVE A RIGHT TO BE WHATEVER THEY WANNA BE AND THAT'S A GOD-GIVEN RIGHT. PEOPLE MUST REMEMBER THAT WE CAN'T BE PREJUDICED AGAINST SOMEONE BECAUSE OF WHAT THEIR CHOICE IS IN LIFE. ALL OF US GOT TO KEEP GOD'S TEN COMMANDMENTS TO MAKE IT IN THE KINGDOM, WHATEVER THE STYLE IS!"

LITTLE RICHARD

"VERY FEW OF MY ALBUMS ARE LOVE SONGS TO ANYONE. MUSIC IS SO BIG, MAN, IT JUST TAKES UP A LOT OF ROOM. I'VE DEDICATED MY LIFE TO MY MUSIC SO FAR. AND EVERY TIME I'VE LET IT SLIP AND GOTTEN SOMEWHERE ELSE, IT'S SHOWED. MUSIC LASTS . . . A LOT LONGER THAN RELATIONSHIPS DO."

NEIL YOUNG

Rolling Stone, August 14, 1975

"I'VE BROKEN TWELVE GUITARS THAT I REALLY LOVED AND I PUT THEM ALL BACK TOGETHER IF THEY COULD BE. ONE I PUT BACK TOGETHER SIX TIMES. THROUGH A PERFORMANCE YOU LEARN TO LOVE A PARTICULAR GUITAR. BREAKING IT IS A WHOLE THING. WHEN YOU BREAK IT, YOU BREAK DOWN YOUR OWN DEPENDENCE ON LOVE OF MATERIAL THINGS."

PETE TOWNSHEND THE WHO

Rolling Stone, January 20, 1968

MADONNA

"EVER SINCE I WAS IN HIGH SCHOOL, WHEN I WAS MADLY IN LOVE WITH SOMEONE, I WAS SO PROUD OF THIS PERSON, I WANTED THE WORLD TO KNOW THAT I LOVED HIM. BUT ONCE YOU REVEAL IT TO THE WORLD—AND YOU'RE IN THE PUBLIC EYE—YOU GIVE IT UP, AND IT'S NOT YOUR OWN ANYMORE. I BEGAN TO REALIZE HOW IMPORTANT IT IS TO HOLD ON TO PRIVACY AND KEEPING THINGS TO YOURSELF AS MUCH AS POSSIBLE. IT'S LIKE A RUNAWAY TRAIN AFTERWARD."

Rolling Stone, March 23, 1989

LOVE AND SEX

MICK JAGGER
THE ROLLING STONES

"OF COURSE I GET LONELY. BUT I DON'T WANT A RELATIONSHIP WITH A WOMAN WHERE I'M IN 'CHARGE' AND I EXPECT FIDELITY AND ALL THAT. I NEVER REQUIRE THAT OF ANYONE, AND I DON'T WANT IT REQUIRED OF ME."

Interview with Lisa Robinson, 1977

"I LIKE BEAUTIFUL WOMEN. I LIKE BEAUTIFUL CARS. I LIKE BEAUTIFUL TREES. I LIKE BEAUTIFUL LANDSCAPES. IT'S NOT A SIN TO APPRECIATE BEAUTY, BUT THAT ISN'T ENOUGH. I WANT SOMEONE WITH SOME FUCKIN' BRAINS, TOO. IF YOU CAN GET THE WHOLE THING, WHY NOT GO FOR IT?"

**DON HENLEY
EAGLES**

Rolling Stone, November 29, 1979

LOVE AND SEX

"THERE WERE LOTS OF NIGHTLY RELATION-SHIPS. BUT THE REASON YOU DON'T WANT TO MAKE A COMMITMENT IS NOT THAT YOU'RE SUCH A FREEWHEELING, ADVENTUROUS PER-SON, IT'S BECAUSE YOU'RE SCARED SHITLESS THAT IT WILL TURN OUT LIKE YOUR MOTHER AND FATHER."

DAVID BOWIE

Interview magazine, May 1990

"HAVE YOU EVER THOUGHT YOU WERE IN LOVE WITH SOMEONE BUT THEN REALIZED YOU WERE JUST STARING IN A MIRROR FOR 20 MINUTES?"

KANYE WEST

LOVE AND SEX

The Independent, November 28, 2010

"...FALLING IN LOVE IS TERRIBLE. IT MAKES YOU ACT FOOLISH, LIKE AN IDIOT. YOU SIGN YOUR LIFE OVER WHEN YOU FALL IN LOVE, AND IT'S AWFUL, IT'S TORTURE. YOU END UP WALKING PAST THEIR HOUSE AT NIGHT AND LOOKING UP LONGINGLY AT THEIR WINDOW... WHO WANTS TO LIVE LIKE THAT?"

LEMMY
MOTÖRHEAD

JOHNNY MARR
THE SMITHS

"YOUR PARTNER SHOULD MAKE YOU BRAVE. AND THAT'S WHAT HAPPENED WITH ME WHEN I WAS 15. I MET THIS GIRL WHO JUST MADE ME BRAVE. I ALREADY WAS ON A MISSION TO DO WHAT I WAS GOING TO DO, AND WE'RE LIKE TWO SIDES OF THE SAME COIN. I THINK THAT A BIT OF IT IS SURVIVAL INSTINCT. IF YOUR WORKING LIFE IS TURBULENT, YOU REALLY NEED YOUR STRUCTURE TO NOT BE TURBULENT. PEOPLE AROUND ME ARE QUITE BOHEMIAN, THEY'RE BY NO MEANS 'STRAIGHT,' AND THAT INCLUDES MY WIFE AND MY MANAGER. WE REALLY BELIEVE IN BOHEMIANISM. BUT AT THE SAME TIME AS BEING BOHEMIAN AND NOT STRAIGHT, MY WIFE AND MY MANAGER ARE SENSIBLE AND DON'T LET ME GET WAY CRAZY."

The Talks, *New York Times*,
October 1, 2014

LOVE AND SEX

JOHN LENNON
THE BEATLES

"I DON'T KNOW WHAT MARRIAGE IS. I HAVE NO IDEA. MARRIAGE HAS NOTHING TO DO WITH A MAN/WOMAN RELATIONSHIP. MY MARRIAGES WERE FOR DIFFERENT REASONS, SO THAT EVEN THOUGH I'VE HAD TWO MARRIAGES THEY HAD NOTHING TO DO WITH EACH OTHER."

Viva, March 1975

"I BELIEVE IN LOVE—BUT NOT PHONEY BULLSHIT LOVE—IT MAKES ME FEEL SICK, IT MAKES ME FEEL BAD TO SEE THESE KIDS WALKING ABOUT IN THE STREETS. IT'S A WASTE OF KIDS. THEY'RE MISGUIDED AND DELUDED. I SEE THEM BLINDLY ACCEPTING ANYTHING OFFERED TO THEM BY THE HIPPIE MACHINE. SING A SONG AND PUT 'LOVE' IN IT AND TAKE A PICTURE OF THE GROUP IN A FLOWER PATCH AND THE KIDS WILL BUY. THE FLOWERS AND LOVE THING IS JUST A NEW WAY OF PACKAGING A PRODUCT."

FRANK ZAPPA

Melody Maker, August 26, 1967

LOVE AND SEX

"I LIKE THE SKY AT NIGHT...AND THE FULL MOON...AND ALL THAT BULLSHIT. MY FAVORITE FLOWER IS POISON IVY."

JOHNNY ROTTEN
SEX PISTOLS

Punk Magazine, March 1977

FIVE GREAT ROCK & ROLL Museums

1. ROCK & ROLL HALL OF FAME (CLEVELAND, OH) —

Established in 1983, the Rock & Roll Hall of Fame ultimately selected Cleveland as its home in 1986. In addition to annually enshrining artists who have been instrumental in the development of Rock & Roll, it features an impressive selection of both permanent and rotating exhibits of musical artifacts, as well as an enormous archive of recorded and written material that spans the history of rock and the various musical forms that inspired and informed it.

2. GRACELAND (MEMPHIS, TN)—

Originally purchased by Elvis Presley in 1957, Graceland was home to the King of Rock & Roll until his untimely death twenty years later. In addition to the mansion, which is largely intact from Elvis's time, there are several other facilities that are part of the property, including a collection of Presley's cars, airplanes, awards, and many stage outfits.

3. STAX MUSEUM OF AMERICAN SOUL MUSIC (MEMPHIS, TN)—

Housed in what was once the home of legendary label Stax Records, the museum opened in 2003 and features

exhibits that chronicle the emergence of soul music from its humble beginnings in gospel to great artists such as Otis Redding, Isaac Hayes, Sam & Dave, Al Green, and many more. Adjacent to the museum is the Stax Music Academy, established to serve at-risk Memphis youth, and the Soulsville Charter School, a tuition-free college preparatory school for more than 600 students.

4. MOTOWN MUSEUM (DETROIT, MI)—Founded in 1959 by

Berry Gordy, Motown Records featured many of the greatest recording artists of the rock era, including Marvin Gaye, the Supremes, Smokey Robinson and the Miracles, Martha Reeves and the Vandellas, the Four Tops, the Jackson Five, Stevie Wonder, and many others. The Motown Museum is housed in the label's former headquarters and recording studio, and features numerous exhibits and memorabilia dedicated to preserving the legacy of "Hitsville USA."

5. BETHEL WOODS CENTER FOR THE ARTS

(BETHEL, NY) —Directly adjacent to where the Woodstock festival was held in 1969, the Bethel Woods Center contains a museum dedicated to the legacy of Woodstock and the sixties with creatively detailed exhibits chronicling the era that spawned the festival, as well as a large collection of music memorabilia and artifacts from the event itself. The arts center hosts an abundant schedule of cultural events and features a large amphitheater that has hosted many performers including Bob Dylan, Hall & Oates, Eagles, Hot Tuna, and John Mayer.

chapter three

INSPIRATION, ADULATION,
and Confidence

Whether they wear their influences on their sleeves or boldly boast about besting their idols, rock stars are usually inspired to make their style of sound by someone, somewhere, or something. What inspires a song, how do performers carry on, and how far do they think they can go? The answers are almost limitless.

The Rock & Roll Wisdom Playlist

Ringo Starr—"I'm the Greatest"
Journey—"Don't Stop Believin'"
Fleetwood Mac—"Dreams"
David Bowie—"Heroes"
Joe Walsh—"Life's Been Good"

JOE STRUMMER
THE CLASH

"AS SOON AS I SAW THEM I KNEW THAT RHYTHM AND BLUES WAS DEAD, THAT THE FUTURE WAS HERE SOMEHOW. EVERY OTHER GROUP WAS RIFFING THEIR WAY THROUGH THE BLACK SABBATH CATALOGUE. BUT HEARING THE (SEX) PISTOLS, I KNEW. I JUST KNEW."

Melody Maker, November 13, 1976

INSPIRATION, ADULATION, AND CONFIDENCE

BRIAN WILSON
THE BEACH BOYS

"THE SOUND OF VOICES WAS ALWAYS MY FAVORITE PART OF A RECORD. BECAUSE THAT'S WHERE THE LOVE IS, IN THE VOICE."

Mojo, March 2004

"MY LIFE WOULD BE MISERABLE IF I DIDN'T HAVE THOSE LITTLE CHUNKS OF DYLAN THOMAS AND T.S. ELIOT. I CAN'T EVEN IMAGINE LIFE WITHOUT THAT STUFF. THOSE ARE THE PAYOFFS: THE FINEST MOMENTS IN MUSIC, THE FINEST MOMENTS IN MOVIES. GREAT MOMENTS ARE PART OF WHAT SUPPORT YOU AS AN ARTIST AND A HUMAN. THEY'RE PART OF WHAT MAKE YOU A HUMAN."

JERRY GARCIA
GRATEFUL DEAD

Rolling Stone, October 31, 1991

INSPIRATION, ADULATION, AND CONFIDENCE

"I GET NO GREATER PLEASURE THAN TO WALK DOWN THE STREET AND HEAR SOMEBODY HUMMING A MELODY THAT I WROTE. THAT'S REALLY GRATIFYING IF YOU HEAR THAT."

PAUL SIMON

Rolling Stone, May 28, 1970

Rolling Stone, June 29, 1978

"I DON'T DREAM MORE THAN ANYBODY ELSE. BUT DREAMS ARE A GREAT INSPIRATION FOR THE LOWLIEST ROCK & ROLL WRITER TO THE GREATEST PLAYWRIGHTS."

MICK JAGGER
THE ROLLING STONES

INSPIRATION, ADULATION, AND CONFIDENCE

Spin, May 1985

"DREAMS ARE FOR WIMPS."

ANTHONY KIEDIS
RED HOT CHILI PEPPERS

GEORGE HARRISON
THE BEATLES

"YOU CAN HEAR SOMETHING AND THINK THAT YOU DON'T LIKE IT, AND THINK THAT IT'S NOT INFLUENCING YOU. BUT YOU ARE WHAT YOU EAT, AND YOU ARE WHAT YOU SEE, WHAT YOU TOUCH, WHAT YOU SMELL AND WHAT YOU HEAR. MUSIC HAS ALWAYS HAD A TRANSCENDENTAL QUALITY INASMUCH AS IT REACHES PARTS OF YOU THAT YOU DON'T EXPECT IT TO REACH. AND IT CAN TOUCH YOU IN A WAY THAT YOU CAN'T EXPRESS. YOU CAN THINK THAT IT HASN'T REACHED YOU, AND YEARS LATER YOU'LL FIND IT COMING OUT."

The Beatles Anthology,
Chronicle Books, 2000

INSPIRATION, ADULATION, AND CONFIDENCE

NICK LOWE

"WHEN YOU START OUT WRITING, YOU REWRITE OTHER PEOPLE'S AND YOUR HERO'S CATALOG. YOU MOVE FROM HERO TO HERO REWRITING THEIR CATALOG. AND THEN ONE DAY YOU'LL USE A BIT OF YOUR LATEST HERO'S CATALOG, BUT YOU'LL PUT IT TOGETHER WITH YOUR SECOND AND THIRD HERO'S CATALOG THAT YOU REWROTE. YOU'LL MIX IT UP. BEFORE YOU KNOW WHAT'S HAPPENING, YOU'VE GOT YOUR OWN STYLE. YOUR OWN STYLE IS A MIXTURE OF EVERYTHING THAT YOU'VE EVER HEARD PUT TOGETHER IN YOUR OWN RECIPE AND YOU DON'T EVEN KNOW YOU'RE DOING IT."

Aquarium Drunkard's *Transmissions*
podcast, July 11, 2017

"YEAH, JUST ABOUT EVERYBODY WHO EXISTS I FIND PLEASURE IN. I LISTEN TO A LOT OF MUSIC AND I SOAK UP EVERYTHING. I'M A GREAT PARASITE MUSICALLY. HOW I INTERPRET WHAT I'VE HEARD IS FOR THE AUDIENCE AND REVIEWER TO DECIDE; BUT I DO KNOW THAT I'M INFLUENCED TERRIBLY BY ANYTHING I LIKE. SOME OF IT CREEPS INTO MY MUSIC, SOME NOT."

Cavalier, January 1973

INSPIRATION, ADULATION, AND CONFIDENCE

"THE BIGGEST MISTAKE IN THE WORLD IS TO THINK THAT YOU HAVE TO EMULATE SOMEBODY ELSE. THAT IS FATAL. IT'S GOT NOTHING TO DO WITH ME. IF PEOPLE WANT TO BE LIKE KEITH RICHARDS, THEN THEY BETTER HAVE THE SAME PHYSICAL MAKEUP. I COME FROM A VERY STURDY STOCK—OTHERWISE I WOULDN'T BE HERE."

KEITH RICHARDS
THE ROLLING STONES

Rolling Stone, October 6, 1988

Rolling Stone, November 13, 1997

"THE IDEA OF A ROLE MODEL GOES AGAINST MY IDEA OF WHY YOU'D GET INTO A BAND. YOU'RE NOT MODELING YOURSELF ON ANYONE."

CHRISSIE HYNDE
THE PRETENDERS

INSPIRATION, ADULATION, AND CONFIDENCE

Describing the creation of "Yesterday",
Paul McCartney: Many Years From Now,
Secker & Warburg, 1997

"I WOKE UP WITH A LOVELY TUNE IN MY HEAD. I THOUGHT, THAT'S GREAT, I WONDER WHAT THAT IS? THERE WAS AN UPRIGHT PIANO NEXT TO ME, TO THE RIGHT OF THE BED BY THE WINDOW. I GOT OUT OF BED, SAT AT THE PIANO, FOUND G, FOUND F SHARP MINOR 7TH—AND THAT LEADS YOU THROUGH THEN TO B TO E MINOR, AND FINALLY BACK TO E. IT ALL LEADS FORWARD LOGICALLY. I LIKED THE MELODY A LOT BUT BECAUSE I'D DREAMED IT I COULDN'T BELIEVE I'D WRITTEN IT. I THOUGHT, NO, I'VE NEVER WRITTEN LIKE THIS BEFORE. BUT I HAD THE TUNE, WHICH WAS THE MOST MAGIC THING. AND YOU HAVE TO ASK YOURSELF, WHERE DID IT COME FROM? BUT YOU DON'T ASK YOURSELF TOO MUCH OR IT MIGHT GO AWAY."

PAUL MCCARTNEY
THE BEATLES

JOHN LENNON
THE BEATLES

"I'M NOT INTERESTED IN SMALL, ELITE GROUPS FOLLOWING OR KOWTOWING TO ME. I'M INTERESTED IN COMMUNICATING WHATEVER IT IS I WANT TO SAY OR PRODUCE IN THE MAXIMUM POSSIBLE WAY, AND ROCK & ROLL IS IT AS FAR AS I'M CONCERNED."

Rolling Stone, December 23, 2010–
January 6, 2011, from an interview with
Jonathan Cott on December 5, 1980

INSPIRATION, ADULATION, AND CONFIDENCE

TOM PETTY

"I NEVER WANTED TO BE A BIG SHOW-BIZ PERSONALITY. I THINK IT'S FINE FOR PEOPLE WHO LIKE IT, BUT IT WOULD TERRIFY ME TO MAKE MY LIFE SO PUBLIC. YOU GET NERVOUS BECAUSE YOU GO PLACES AND YOU START TO DRAW A CROWD. PEOPLE NEVER DO ANYTHING TO YOU. IT'S MORE LIKE, 'HI, TOM. LOVE YOUR ALBUM. WILL YOU SIGN THIS?' AND THAT'S FINE. BUT IT'S STILL EMBARRASSING TO BE STANDING IN LINE FOR A MOVIE AND EVERYONE STARTS TO SHOUT."

Trouser Press, August 1981

"MAN, IT WAS JUST A PURE, JOYFUL, INDEPENDENT SPIRIT...WHEN PUNK CAME, IT WAS LIKE, 'SHIT, I CAN RELATE TO THAT. I CAN PICK UP MY BASS AND DO THAT, THAT CAN BE MY VOICE.' IT MADE ME FREE, OH, COMPLETELY. IT WAS AN ENERGY THAT HAD NEVER BEEN TRANSLATED INTO MUSIC BEFORE. AND IT WASN'T ABOUT FANTASY AND ENTERTAINMENT, IT WAS REAL."

JEFF AMENT
PEARL JAM

Uncut, December 2002

INSPIRATION, ADULATION, AND CONFIDENCE

84

"YOU JUST HAD TO OPEN THE BACK DOOR AND THERE IT WAS. THE NEIGHBORS HAD ALL THE HANK WILLIAMS STUFF, SO I HEARD THAT FROM FIVE DOORS DOWN. THERE WERE A LOT OF MUSICIANS IN THE AREA. PEOPLE HAD ALL THESE GREAT RECORDS. NOT JUST MY DAD BUT ALL MY FRIENDS. WHEREVER YOU WENT, THERE WAS THIS GREAT MUSIC."

VAN MORRISON

Uncut, July 2005

Guitar World, November 2008

"I REMEMBER THE FIRST THREE LIVE SHOWS I EVER SAW: STIFF LITTLE FINGERS, RORY GALLAGHER, THE CLASH. TALK ABOUT HAVING YOUR MIND BLOWN. I FELT THE SAME WAY WHEN I SAW SPRINGSTEEN FOR THE FIRST TIME. IT WAS LIKE HAVING MY EYES OPENED FOR THE FIRST TIME. IT WAS A CATHARSIS, AND THAT'S WHAT WE TRY TO BRING TO EVERY SHOW WE PLAY."

THE EDGE
U2

INSPIRATION, ADULATION, AND CONFIDENCE

Mojo, November 2005

"WE WERE LIKE THE BEATLES ON SPEED. OR, IF YOU WERE A READER OF SUPER-MAN COMICS, WE WERE A BIZARRO WORLD VERSION OF THE BEATLES."

TOMMY RAMONE
RAMONES

LIAM GALLAGHER
OASIS

"THOSE FIRST TWO ALBUMS, *DEFINITELY MAYBE* AND *(WHAT'S THE STORY) MORNING GLORY*, ARE THE BOLLOCKS, MAN. THERE ISN'T A BAND IN HISTORY WHOSE FIRST TWO ALBUMS WERE THAT GOOD."

Q, October 2014

INSPIRATION, ADULATION, AND CONFIDENCE

GENE SIMMONS
KISS

"FROM THE START, WE KNEW WE WANTED TO MAKE MUSIC THAT CAME FROM THE CROTCH AND NOT THE CRANIUM. QUITE SIMPLY, WE WANTED TO MAKE LOUD ROCK'N'ROLL THAT WASN'T SO COMPLICATED THAT IT STOPPED US FROM RUNNING AROUND ONSTAGE. ONCE THE MUSIC, THE BAND NAME, THE LOGO AND THE MAKE-UP WAS IN PLACE, WE HAD AN UNSHAKEABLE CONFIDENCE THAT IT WAS GOING TO WORK AND IT WAS GOING TO BE HUGE. EVEN WHEN WE WERE PLAYING TO THREE PEOPLE IN THE MIDDLE OF NOWHERE. TO ME, THE IDEA OF BEING IN A BAND AND NOT WANTING TO BE MEGA, THAT WAS IDIOTIC."

Uncut, March 2006

"IF YOU CAN'T HOLD TWO IDEAS IN YOUR HEAD AT THE SAME TIME, YOU'RE NOT GOING TO GET WHAT I DO."

FATHER JOHN MISTY

The New Yorker, June 26, 2017

INSPIRATION, ADULATION, AND CONFIDENCE

"IT'S A PRETTY BIG WORLD OUT THERE, AND IT'S PRETTY TEPID. IT'S LIKE A KETTLE INTO AN OCEAN, ISN'T IT? MY PLAN IS TO MAKE A MUSICAL METEOR THE SIZE OF THE FUCKING MOON THAT RADIATES ATOMIC HEAT AS IT SHEDS PROTONS, THAT PLOUGHS INTO THE PACIFIC OCEAN KILLING EVERYTHING IN ITS PATH EXCEPT A SINGLE BUTTERFLY THAT PLAYS BASS LIKE JEAN JACQUES BURNEL FROM THE STRANGLERS."

JAMES MURPHY
LCD SOUNDSYSTEM

Uncut, February 2005

Spin, January 2003

"FROM THE BEGINNING, OUR GOAL WAS TO MAKE SOMETHING THAT WAS LESS POPULAR BUT THAT WOULD BE APPRECIATED LATER."

JULIAN CASABLANCAS
THE STROKES

INSPIRATION, ADULATION, AND CONFIDENCE

The Talks, *New York Times*,
November 5, 2013

"OF COURSE WHEN WE STARTED OUT I THOUGHT THE MUSIC
WE WERE DOING WAS GOOD AND THAT WE WERE GOING
TO REPLACE ALL THE DINOSAURS. BUT I ALSO REALIZED
THAT THE DINOSAURS ARE REALLY GOOD, SOME OF THEM
ARE REALLY GOOD—ALL OF THESE BANDS, WHETHER IT'S
FLEETWOOD MAC OR WHOEVER—AND I AM NOT SO GOOD SO
I THOUGHT, 'NO, NOT LIKELY.'"

DAVID BYRNE
TALKING HEADS

IGGY POP

"YEAH, I'D LIKE TO BE A MOVIE STAR...AND A ROCK & ROLL STAR...AND OWN A COUPLE OF BANKS, AND BE A MASTER CRIMINAL, AND FUCK DIVORCEES UPTOWN, AND, YA KNOW, JUST DO EVERYTHING. I HAVE ALL THE DESIRES."

Punk Magazine, July 1976

INSPIRATION, ADULATION, AND CONFIDENCE

JOHNNY ROTTEN
SEX PISTOLS

"I NEVER UNDERSTOOD WHY PEOPLE ARE SCARED TO GO ON A STAGE, 'CAUSE IT DOESN'T TAKE ANYTHING. YOU DON'T HAVE TO BE DRUNK OR OUT OF YOUR HEAD. JUST WALK UP THERE. THAT IS IF YOU FEEL LIKE DOING IT."

Punk Magazine, March 1977

"I HAVE NO CONTROL OVER THE AUDIENCE. I HAVE NO IDEA WHAT THEY THINK. MY HEART'S PURE, I CAN'T DO ANYTHING. I REALLY CAN'T DO ANYTHING. I DON'T KNOW WHAT GOES ON IN THE CROWD. I'VE HAD THEM SHOW UP AND THROW BEER CANS AT ME. I CAUSED RIOTS IN MOST OF THE MAJOR CITIES. WHAT CAN I DO?"

Spin, November 2008

INSPIRATION, ADULATION, AND CONFIDENCE

"I WANT TO REALLY COMMUNICATE WITH PEOPLE AND TOUCH HUMANITY AND COMPLETE MY CREATIVE PROCESS AND BECOME A COMPLETE ARTIST. PROJECT A REALITY, A SENSE OF ART. I THINK ART SHOULD REFLECT LIFE. ARTISTS HAVE A RESPONSIBILITY TO DO THAT, YOU KNOW."

CYNDI LAUPER

Smash Hits, February 2-15, 1984

Rolling Stone, March 13, 1975

"BOREDOM IS A HORRIBLE THING. BOREDOM IS THE BEGINNING OF ALL DESTRUCTION AND EVERYTHING THAT IS NEGATIVE."

ROBERT PLANT
LED ZEPPELIN

INSPIRATION, ADULATION, AND CONFIDENCE

Rolling Stone, March 13, 1975

"SO MANY PEOPLE ARE FRIGHTENED TO TAKE A CHANCE IN LIFE AND THERE'S SO MANY CHANCES YOU HAVE TO TAKE. YOU CAN'T JUST FIND YOURSELF DOING SOMETHING AND NOT HAPPY DOING IT. IF YOU'RE WORKING AT THE FACTORY AND YOU'RE CURSING EVERY DAY THAT YOU GET UP, AT ALL COSTS GET OUT OF IT. YOU'LL JUST MAKE YOURSELF ILL. THAT'S WHY I SAY I'M VERY FORTUNATE BECAUSE I LOVE WHAT I'M DOING. SEEING PEOPLE'S FACES, REALLY GETTING OFF ON THEM, MAKES ME INCREDIBLY HAPPY. GENUINELY."

JIMMY PAGE
LED ZEPPELIN

MICHAEL JACKSON

"MAGIC IS EASY IF YOU PUT YOUR HEART INTO IT."

Creem, June 1983

INSPIRATION, ADULATION, AND CONFIDENCE

BRIAN WILSON
THE BEACH BOYS

"(I)F YOU SPEND YOUR LIFE TRYING TO FIND SONGS, YOU REALIZE PRETTY QUICKLY THAT YOU'RE NOT THE FIRST. PEOPLE HAVE BEEN DOING THAT AS LONG AS THERE HAVE BEEN PEOPLE. AND IF THERE ARE PERIODS IN YOUR LIFE WHEN YOU STOP DOING IT—BECAUSE SOMETHING DISTRACTS YOU OR MAKES YOU WEAK—YOU REALIZE HOW IMPORTANT IT IS TO JUMP RIGHT BACK INTO THE GAME. SONGS ARE OUT THERE ALL THE TIME, BUT THEY CAN'T BE MADE WITHOUT PEOPLE. YOU HAVE TO DO YOUR JOB AND HELP SONGS COME INTO EXISTENCE."

I Am Brian Wilson: A Memoir,
Da Capo Press, 2016

"TO INSPIRE PEOPLE, EVEN FOR JUST ONE SECOND, IS WORTH SOMETHING. TO BE HONEST, WE WERE BLOKES WITH GUITARS, AND IT'S UNLIKELY WE COULD CHANGE THE WORLD, BUT AT EIGHTEEN, YOU AT LEAST THINK IT'S POSSIBLE—AND IT IS, BUT MAYBE NOT IN THE WAY YOU FIRST THINK."

PAUL SIMONON
THE CLASH

3:AM Magazine, November 2004

INSPIRATION, ADULATION, AND CONFIDENCE

"A LOT OF POP MUSIC HAS COME OUT OF PEOPLE FAILING TO COPY THEIR MODEL AND ACCIDENTALLY CREATING SOMETHING NEW. THE CLOSER YOU GET TO YOUR IDEAL, THE LESS ORIGINAL YOU SOUND."

ELVIS COSTELLO

Unfaithful Music & Disappearing Ink,
Blue Rider Press, 2015

Chronicles: Volume One,
Simon & Schuster, 2004

"CREATIVITY HAS MUCH TO DO WITH EXPERIENCE, OBSERVATION AND IMAGINATION, AND IF ANY ONE OF THOSE KEY ELEMENTS IS MISSING, IT DOESN'T WORK."

BOB DYLAN

INSPIRATION, ADULATION, AND CONFIDENCE

Born to Run, Simon & Schuster, 2016

"I'D SEEN OTHER GREAT MUSICIANS LOSE THEIR WAY AND WATCH THEIR MUSIC AND ART BECOME ANEMIC, ROOT-LESS, DISPLACED WHEN THEY SEEMED TO LOSE TOUCH WITH WHO THEY WERE. MY MUSIC WOULD BE A MUSIC OF IDENTITY, A SEARCH FOR MEANING AND THE FUTURE."

BRUCE SPRINGSTEEN

NEIL YOUNG

"MY LIFE IS NOT A POLITICAL CAMPAIGN. I JUST WRITE ABOUT WHAT IS ON MY MIND. I JUST PLAY WHATEVER I FEEL LIKE PLAYING. WHATEVER IS IN MY SOUL AT THE TIME IS WHAT I WANT TO DO. I HAVE, THANK GOD, ENOUGH PEOPLE WHO ARE STILL INTERESTED IN WHAT I AM DOING SO THAT I CAN GO OUT AND KEEP DOING IT."

The Talks, *New York Times*,
April 18, 2013

INSPIRATION, ADULATION, AND CONFIDENCE

NICK CAVE

"TO BE HONEST I FEEL THAT IF I AM NOT CREATING MY SENSE OF SELF PLUMMETS SO LOW, MY FEELINGS ABOUT MYSELF AND MY SELF-ESTEEM TAKE SUCH A RAPID NOSE-DIVE, THAT I HAVE TO GET BACK IN THE GAME AND START DOING SOMETHING AGAIN JUST TO FEEL LIKE I AM ENGAGED IN THE WORLD."

The Talks, *New York Times*,
January 4, 2012

"I'M NOT REALLY A MUSICIAN. I'M A PERFORMER AND I LOVE ROCK & ROLL. I'VE EMBRACED ROCK & ROLL BECAUSE IT ENCOMPASSES ALL THE THINGS I'M INTERESTED IN: POETRY, REVOLUTION, SEXUALITY, POLITICAL ACTIVISM—ALL OF THESE THINGS CAN BE FOUND IN ROCK & ROLL. BUT I AM ALSO ENGAGED IN ALL OF THESE THINGS SEPARATELY. I DON'T HAVE AN IMAGE OF MYSELF, WHEN I'M WALKING DOWN THE STREET, LIKE I'M A ROCK STAR OR SOMETHING. I'M A HUMAN BEING, I'M A FRIEND, I'M A MOM, I'M A WRITER, AND I'M AN ARTIST. I DO PLAY ELECTRIC GUITAR AND ALL OF THAT BUT IN THE END I'M JUST A PERSON."

PATTI SMITH

The Talks, *New York Times*, June 22, 2011

INSPIRATION, ADULATION, AND CONFIDENCE

108

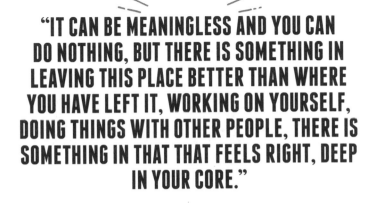

"IT CAN BE MEANINGLESS AND YOU CAN DO NOTHING, BUT THERE IS SOMETHING IN LEAVING THIS PLACE BETTER THAN WHERE YOU HAVE LEFT IT, WORKING ON YOURSELF, DOING THINGS WITH OTHER PEOPLE, THERE IS SOMETHING IN THAT THAT FEELS RIGHT, DEEP IN YOUR CORE."

ALBERT HAMMOND, JR.
THE STROKES

The Talks, *New York Times*,
October 10, 2013

Pulse!, June 1996

"I THINK IT'S A WASTE OF TIME, THAT WHOLE ROCK-STAR CLICHÉ THING. IF YOU'RE LUCKY ENOUGH TO DO SOMETHING LIKE THIS, THERE'S A CERTAIN INHERENT GRACIOUSNESS YOU HAVE TO MAINTAIN."

INSPIRATION, ADULATION, AND CONFIDENCE

Interview with Legs McNeil conducted
in 1989, published online on
Pleasekillme.com on December 6, 2017

"I THINK ROCK & ROLL SHOULD BE THREE WORDS AND A CHORUS. AND THE THREE WORDS SHOULD BE GOOD ENOUGH TO SAY IT ALL."

DEE DEE RAMONE
RAMONES

BEST ACTING
PERFORMANCES BY
Rock Stars

1. ELVIS PRESLEY IN *KING CREOLE*—Though he appeared in over 30 films, Elvis Presley is most likely remembered for movies like *Jailhouse Rock* or *Viva Las Vegas*. But it was the King's fourth film, *King Creole*, that was his favorite, a dramatic turn which he felt gave him his best opportunity to follow in the footsteps of actors like James Dean and Marlon Brando. Elvis plays Danny Fisher, a troubled New Orleans teen who falls in with the wrong crowd. He sings, he gyrates, but, unlike many of his later films, Elvis is given an opportunity to act too. He makes the most of it.

2. ART GARFUNKEL IN *CARNAL KNOWLEDGE*—Best known as the taller half of folk-rock duo Simon & Garfunkel, Art Garfunkel's forays into cinema have been few. His best work came in the Mike Nichols-directed 1971 film *Carnal Knowledge*, a comic-drama co-starring Jack Nicholson, Candice Bergen and Ann-Margret. As Sandy, Garfunkel is the quiet, awkwardly sensitive counterpoint to Nicholson's Jonathan, a bold misogynist. Garfunkel's performance is understated and genuine during the three periods of Sandy's life seen on screen, and he received a nomination for the Golden Globe Award for Best Supporting Actor for the role.

3. COURTNEY LOVE IN *THE PEOPLE VS. LARRY FLYNT*—In director Milos Forman's 1996 biographical drama *The People vs. Larry Flynt*, Hole founder Courtney Love played Althea Leasure, a stripper who would go on to marry *Hustler* magazine founder Flynt. As Leasure, Love portrays a wily and shrewd young woman who would go on to run a successful business, succumb to addiction, the ravages of AIDS, and an eventual death by drowning in a bathtub. Love won numerous awards for her performance, and was also nominated for the Golden Globe Award for Best Supporting Actress.

4. CHER IN *MOONSTRUCK*—Cher shines as lovesick widow Loretta Castorini in Norman Jewison's 1987 romantic comedy *Moonstruck*, a role which earned her many accolades, including both the Academy Award and Golden Globe Award for best actress. Torn between tradition and her love for her fiancé's estranged younger brother, Cher as Loretta is wild, over the top, and totally believable. *Moonstruck* is high on numerous lists by the American Film Institute, in large part due to Cher's performance in a stellar ensemble cast.

5. DAVID BOWIE IN *THE MAN WHO FELL TO EARTH*—
Though David Bowie had already established himself as an otherworldly performer in the Rock & Roll idiom, it wasn't until his debut starring role in Nicolas Roeg's 1976 psychological sci-fi film that he actually played an alien. As Thomas Jerome Newton, the stranded humanoid alien, Bowie reveals layers of vulnerability and, ultimately, humanity.

chapter four
INTEGRITY AND
Work Ethic

The struggle between creativity and commerce, the tussle between art and artifice, and the invaluable component of plain hard work, are common themes in Rock & Roll. Rock's unique ability to bend and break the rules hasn't helped make things any clearer in all the years either. The beat goes on.

The Rock & Roll Wisdom Playlist

Dire Straits—"Money for Nothing"
Neil Young—"This Note's For You"
Elvis Costello—"Welcome to the Working Week"
John Lennon—"Gimme Some Truth"
The Clash—"Complete Control"

JOE STRUMMER
THE CLASH

"WE'RE HERE TO DO ONE JOB—PLAY THE GIG. THAT'S WHAT WE SHOULD BE CONCENTRATING ON. WHAT WE SHOULD BE DOING IS GOING OUT AND PLAYING THE BEST ROCK & ROLL SHOW THESE PEOPLE HAVE EVER SEEN AND PISS OFF."

Melody Maker, February 24, 1979

INTEGRITY AND WORK ETHIC

JIM MORRISON
THE DOORS

"IN A CONCERT SITUATION, YOU CAN'T REALLY LOSE. YOU GET THAT MANY PEOPLE TOGETHER AND IT DOESN'T MATTER SO MUCH WHAT YOU DO. IN A CLUB YOU HAVE TO TURN PEOPLE ON MUSICALLY. IF IT DOESN'T CUT IT, EVERYONE KNOWS IT."

Rolling Stone, July 26, 1969

"I GUESS ANY ARTIST, IF THE AUDIENCE ACTS LIKE THEY'RE ENJOYING IT, IF THEY ACT LIKE THEY'RE WITH YOU, IT MAKES YOU PUT MORE INTO IT, YOU KNOW?"

ELVIS PRESLEY

Hy Gardner Calling, 1956

INTEGRITY AND WORK ETHIC

"I DON'T WAKE UP IN THE MORNING AND SAY: 'JEEZ, I FEEL GREAT TODAY. I THINK I'LL WRITE A SONG.' I MEAN, ANYTHING IS MORE INTERESTING TO ME THAN WRITING A SONG. IT'S LIKE 'I THINK I'D LIKE TO WRITE A SONG.... NO, I GUESS I BETTER GO FEED THE CAT FIRST.' YOU KNOW WHAT I MEAN? IT'S LIKE PULLING TEETH. I DON'T ENJOY IT A BIT."

JERRY GARCIA
GRATEFUL DEAD

Rolling Stone, October 31, 1991

Interview by Howard Smith, fall 1969.
From *The Smith Tapes: Lost Interviews with
Rock Stars & Icons 1969–1972*,
Princeton Architectural Press, 2015

"IT'S A DISCIPLINARY THING WHERE YOU SAY, 'WELL, I'M GONNA WRITE AT TWO O'CLOCK TODAY.' AND YOU GET TOGETHER WITH WHOMEVER YOU'RE WRITING WITH AND YOU SAY, 'WELL, LET'S SIT DOWN AND SEE IF WE CAN COME UP WITH SOMETHING,' AND YOU THROW IDEAS AROUND AND VERY OFTEN SOMETHING DOES COME OUT. EVEN IF YOU DON'T PARTICULARLY FEEL LIKE WRITING THAT DAY OR AT THAT PARTICULAR TIME, IF YOU DO IT LONG ENOUGH, YOU KNOW HOW TO MAKE YOURSELF GET REALLY TURNED ON AND YOU DO IT. IT WORKS."

CAROLE KING

INTEGRITY AND WORK ETHIC

Rolling Stone, March 23, 1989

"DEEP DOWN INSIDE, I'M A REALLY NICE GIRL. BUT, CERTAINLY, I CAN BE A BITCH. I'M A PER-FECTIONIST, AND I'M UNDER LOTS OF PRES-SURE. SOMETIMES YOU HAVE TO BE A BITCH TO GET THINGS DONE."

MADONNA

BOB DYLAN

"ALL I CAN DO IS BE ME—WHOEVER THAT IS—FOR THOSE PEOPLE THAT I DO PLAY TO, AND NOT COME ON WITH THEM, TELL THEM SOMETHING I'M NOT. I'M NOT GOING TO TELL THEM I'M THE GREAT CAUSE FIGHTER OR THE GREAT LOVER, OR THE GREAT BOY GENIUS OR WHATEVER. BECAUSE I'M NOT, MAN. WHY MISLEAD THEM? THAT'S ALL JUST MADISON AVENUE SELLING ME, BUT IT'S NOT REALLY SELLING ME, 'CAUSE I WAS HIP TO IT BEFORE I GOT THERE."

L.A. Free Press, March 1965

INTEGRITY AND WORK ETHIC

JAMES BROWN

"ANYONE WHO WORKS FOR ME HAS GOT TO WORK HARD, OR ELSE THEY AREN'T STRONG ENOUGH TO BE A PART OF THE JAMES BROWN REVUE. I'VE NEVER BEEN AFRAID OF HARD WORK. IN FACT, I'M PROUD OF IT. I'VE BEEN CALLED THE HARDEST-WORKING MAN IN SHOW BUSINESS. I LIKE THAT NAME BECAUSE IT SIGNIFIES A CONNECTION TO MY BLUE-COLLAR ROOTS AND DEFINES THE INTENSITY OF THE WORK THAT GOES INTO MAKING MY MUSIC."

I Feel Good: A Memoir of a Life in Soul,
New American Library, 2005

"I JUST LIKE ATTRACTIVE PRESENTATION. I ALWAYS HAVE DONE, WHETHER IT'S IN A BOOK JACKET, AN ALBUM SLEEVE OR A STAGE PERFORMANCE. ONE OF THE BEST SHOWS I EVER SAW WAS THE OTIS REDDING TOUR WITH ALL THESE STAX PEOPLE, AND THEY WERE LOOKING IMMACULATE IN THEIR OUTFITS, AND ALL PLAYING AND MOVING TIGHTLY. YOU CAN EITHER DO A THING WELL OR NOT BOTHER TO TRY."

**BRYAN FERRY
ROXY MUSIC**

Creem, June 1975

INTEGRITY AND WORK ETHIC

"AND I DON'T BELIEVE IN TOMORROWS, THAT 'OH, I'LL PUT THE OTHER HALF OUT SIX MONTHS FROM NOW.' YOU MAY BE DEAD, YOU JUST DON'T KNOW. YOU MAKE YOUR RECORDS LIKE IT'S THE LAST RECORD YOU'LL EVER MAKE. YOU GO OUT AND PLAY AT NIGHT. I DON'T THINK 'IF I DON'T PLAY GOOD TONIGHT AT LEAST I PLAYED GOOD LAST NIGHT.' IT'S LIKE, THERE ARE NO TOMORROWS OR YESTERDAYS. THERE'S ONLY RIGHT NOW."

BRUCE SPRINGSTEEN

Creem, January 1981

Uncut, July 2005

"YOU HAVE TO UNDERSTAND THAT I DON'T CHOOSE THE MUSIC; IT CHOOSES ME. MY LOVE FOR THE MUSIC IS THE CORE OF IT FOR ME. MAYBE THERE'S PEOPLE WHO DO MUSIC FOR DIFFERENT REASONS. FINANCIAL REASONS OR EGO REASONS. MAYBE THEY CAN WALK AWAY FROM IT. BUT I CAN'T. BECAUSE MY CONNECTION TO THE MUSIC CAN'T BE BROKEN. THIS IS A NEED. LET'S BE CLEAR ABOUT THIS—THERE IS NO FUCKING CHOICE."

VAN MORRISON

INTEGRITY AND WORK ETHIC

The Talks, *New York Times*,
November 21, 2017

"I THINK YOU KNOW WHEN YOU'RE PLAYING IT SAFE, WHEN YOU'RE STAGNATING, AND WHEN YOU'RE GROWING. IT'S PROBABLY AN ONGOING THING FOR ALL OF US—AND A TRICKY BALANCE. OBVIOUSLY IT'S IMPORTANT TO NOT OVERREACH OR YOU RISK BYPASSING FERTILE MOMENTS, BUT I DO TRY TO LEARN AT LEAST ONE THING ON EVERY ALBUM, TO REACH OUT IN TERMS OF SOFTWARE OR GROWING IN MY ARRANGEMENTS, OR I PROBABLY TEND TO WRITE HARDER AND HARDER MELODIES FOR ME TO SING. I BECOME MY OWN TEACHER."

BJÖRK

DAVID BOWIE

"I REFUSE TO BE THOUGHT OF AS MEDIOCRE. IF I AM MEDIOCRE, I'LL GET OUT OF THE BUSINESS. THERE'S ENOUGH FOG AROUND. THAT'S WHY THE IDEA OF PERFORMANCE-AS-SPECTACLE IS SO IMPORTANT TO ME."

Rolling Stone, April 1, 1971

INTEGRITY AND WORK ETHIC

TOM WAITS

"ACHIEVEMENT IS FOR SENATORS AND SCHOLARS. AT ONE TIME I HAD AMBITIONS BUT I HAD THEM REMOVED BY A DOCTOR IN BUFFALO. IT STARTED AS A CYST, IT GREW UNDER MY ARM AND I HAD TO HAVE NEW SHIRTS MADE, IT WAS AWFUL. BUT I HAVE THEM IN A JAR AT HOME NOW."

NME, October 19, 1985

"...THE FACT ABOUT IT IS THAT YOU DIDN'T GO AROUND SAYING, 'I HAD THE WORK ETHIC.' IT'S JUST WHAT PEOPLE DID. PEOPLE DIDN'T HAVE TIME TO THINK ABOUT WHAT IT IS: YOU EITHER DID IT OR YOU DIDN'T DO IT. THERE WAS NO TIME FOR PONDERING. I FIND IN RETROSPECT A LOT OF IT IS ROMANTICIZED, AND MYTHOLOGIZED, BUT EARLY ON THERE WASN'T ANY OF THAT. IT'S A JOB LIKE ANY OTHER JOB, AND IF YOU WANTED TO DO IT, AND LOVED DOING IT, THEN IT WAS A GOOD JOB. SO THAT'S THE WAY YOU LOOKED AT IT."

VAN MORRISON

The Irish Times, August 29, 2015

INTEGRITY AND WORK ETHIC

"I UNDERSTAND LIFE NOW I THINK, AND I UNDERSTAND WORK AND I THINK UNDERSTANDING WORK IS FAR BIGGER THAN UNDERSTANDING LIFE BECAUSE WORK IS REALLY WHAT KEEPS ONE LIVING."

PETE TOWNSHEND
THE WHO

International Times, February 13-26, 1967

Born to Run, Simon & Schuster, 2016

"I LEARNED THAT UNLESS YOU ARE VERY AGGRESSIVE, VERY PROACTIVE ABOUT WHAT YOU WANT, WHAT YOU'VE CREATED CAN BE CO-OPTED AND TAKEN FROM YOU, WHATEVER THE RESULTS. IT'S NOTHING PERSONAL. YOU WILL SIMPLY BE STRIPPED BARE, FOR BETTER OR WORSE, AT THE ALTAR OF THE GREAT MARKETING GODS, WHO HAVE A DYNAMIC AND AN AGENDA GUIDED BY THE DNA OF COMMERCE."

BRUCE SPRINGSTEEN

INTEGRITY AND WORK ETHIC

132

Rolling Stone, November 13, 1997

"AT THE VERY EARLY SHOWS, WHEN WE DIDN'T HAVE MUCH IN THE WAY OF DRESSING ROOMS AND THE GUYS COULD MAYBE PISS IN A SINK IF WE COULDN'T GET TO A TOILET, I'D HAVE TO ASK THEM TO TURN AROUND WHILE I WOULD PISS IN A PINT MUG. THEN I FELT ALIENATED-SLASH-EMBARRASSED."

CHRISSIE HYNDE
THE PRETENDERS

OZZY OSBOURNE

"...UNLIKE A LOT OF THE ONE-HIT-WONDER TOP-FORTY BANDS AT THE TIME, WE WEREN'T FAKE. WE HADN'T BEEN PUT TOGETHER BY SOME SUIT-AND-TIE IN A SMOKY OFFICE IN LONDON SOMEWHERE. WE WEREN'T ONE STAR, A COOL NAME, AND A BUNCH OF SESSION PLAYERS WHO CHANGED WITH EVERY TOUR. WE WERE THE REAL FUCKING DEAL."

I Am Ozzy,
Grand Central Publishing, 2010

INTEGRITY AND WORK ETHIC

TOPPER HEADON
THE CLASH

"I THINK EVERY BAND HAS A SHELF LIFE.
WE NEVER GREW OLD ON THE STAGE.
WE HAD FIVE YEARS, WE RELEASED ALL
THAT MATERIAL, TOURED INCESSANTLY,
AND THEN IMPLODED RIGHT AT THE TOP."

The Clash on the Clash: Interviews and Encounters, *Chicago Review Press*, 2017

"...ULTIMATELY YOU HAVE TO DO WHAT YOU DO FOR YOURSELF. I THINK THERE IS A LOT OF MUSIC THAT IS QUITE PRODUCT-ORIENTED AND THERE ISN'T ANYTHING WRONG WITH THAT. CERTAIN MUSIC IS FINE WITH THAT—THREE MINUTE SONGS AND THESE TYPES OF DYNAMICS THAT MAKE THEM MORE ACCEPTABLE FOR THE RADIO, FOR MASS MEDIA. WE JUST NEVER REALLY PLAYED THAT GIG. WHEN YOU TRY TO SELL A PRODUCT, YOU MAKE IT AS APPEALING TO AS MANY PEOPLE AS POSSIBLE SO YOU CAN SELL AS MUCH OF YOUR PRODUCT AS POSSIBLE AND THAT IS NOT THE WAY WE HAVE EVER LOOKED AT WHAT WE DO. IF WE WANTED TO SELL A PRODUCT, WE COULD JUST SELL TOOTHPASTE."

LARS ULRICH
METALLICA

The Talks, *New York Times*,
November 21, 2013

INTEGRITY AND WORK ETHIC

136

SIX KEY
ROCK & ROLL
Festivals

1. MONTEREY INTERNATIONAL POP FESTIVAL, Monterey, California (June 16-18, 1967)—Though it was preceded by the Fantasy Fair and Magic Mountain Music Festival held a week earlier, the Monterey International Pop Festival is still viewed as the gold standard of the Californian Aquarian ideal. Held on the Monterey County Fairgrounds, the festival featured now-legendary performances by the Who, Janis Joplin, the Jefferson Airplane, the Mamas and the Papas, Grateful Dead, Otis Redding, and the Jimi Hendrix Experience.

2. WOODSTOCK MUSIC & ART FAIR, Bethel, New York (August 15-17, 1969)—With an estimated 400,000 people in attendance, the Woodstock Music & Art Fair was billed as "An Aquarian Exposition: 3 Days of Peace & Music." Long considered a countercultural tentpole, the festival included sets by Sly & the Family Stone, the Who, the Band, and the second-ever show by Crosby, Stills, Nash & Young.

3. GLASTONBURY, Worthy Farm, Pilton, Somerset, England—Founded in 1970, Glastonbury has grown from around 1,500 attendees in its inaugural year to roughly

135,000 today. Generally held over five days, the festival boasts around 100 performers across numerous stages each year, with acts representing a wide range of musical styles and eras. Recent headliners include the Rolling Stones, Neil Young, Bruce Springsteen, Foo Fighters, and Metallica.

4. US FESTIVAL, Glen Helen Regional Park, San Bernardino, California (September 3-5, 1982, and May 28-30 and June 4, 1983)—Concocted by Apple cofounder Steve Wozniak, the US Festival was intended to be a celebration of technology and music. Held only twice, the US Festival featured big name performers in 1982 like Talking Heads, the Police, Tom Petty & the Heartbreakers, Fleetwood Mac, and the Cars. In its second and final year, each day's lineup was themed, beginning with New Wave Day and performances by INXS, Men at Work, Stray Cats, and the final show by the Clash to feature founding guitarist Mick Jones. The focus on the remaining days shifted to Heavy Metal (Van Halen, Ozzy Osbourne, Mötley Crüe), Rock (David Bowie, U2, Joe Walsh, Stevie Nicks), and Country (Willie Nelson, Waylon Jennings, Emmylou Harris).

5. LOLLAPALOOZA, Grant Park, Chicago, Illinois—Lollapalooza began life as a summer tour during the nineties heyday of "alternative" music, it's since settled into a permanent annual location in Chicago's Grant Park. Cofounded by Jane's Addiction frontman Perry Farrell, the festival's touring years included performers like Red Hot Chili Peppers, Beastie Boys, Nine Inch Nails, and Soundgarden. In addition to the multi-stage Chicago-based iteration, Lollapalooza has

expanded to hold festivals around the world in countries like Chile, Brazil, Argentina, France, and Germany.

6. COACHELLA VALLEY MUSIC AND ARTS FESTIVAL, Empire Polo Club, Indio, California—Founded in 1999, Coachella is the American equivalent of Glastonbury, in decidedly less muddy environs. With big name headliners and emerging acts alike, Coachella has grown to allow for around a quarter million music fans to enjoy the annual April festival, held over two weekends since 2013. Paul McCartney, Prince, Roger Waters, Guns N' Roses, and AC/DC have all headlined Coachella over the years.

chapter five
FAMILY AND
Friendship

Though the life of a traveling musician can seem ideal for lone wolves, many rock stars find the pull of domesticity irresistible. Others sometimes form strong familial bonds within their own bands, becoming almost brothers and sisters to one another. Whether their siblings are by birth or design, rock stars all came from

somewhere, many of them following their course because of the influence, good or bad, of parents or guardians.

The Rock & Roll Wisdom Playlist

The Pretenders—"I'll Stand By You"
John Lennon—"Mother"
Neil Young—"Old Man"
The White Stripes—"We're Going to Be Friends"
Cyndi Lauper—"True Colors"

Chronicles: Volume One,
Simon & Schuster, 2004

"MY FAMILY WAS MY LIGHT AND I WAS GOING TO PROTECT THAT LIGHT AT ALL COST. THAT WAS WHERE MY DEDICATION WAS, FIRST, LAST AND EVERYTHING IN-BETWEEN. WHAT DID I OWE THE REST OF THE WORLD? NOTHING. NOT A DAMN THING."

BOB DYLAN

FAMILY AND FRIENDSHIP

"I WASN'T CLOSE TO MY MOTHER OR FATHER. AND THAT'S WHY, WHEN IT ALL WENT WRONG—WHEN MY MOTHER DIED—I FELT A REAL RESENTMENT, BECAUSE I ACTUALLY HAD NEVER GOT A CHANCE . . . TO FEEL THAT UNCONDITIONAL LOVE A MOTHER HAS FOR A CHILD. THERE WAS A FEELING OF THAT HOUSE PULLED DOWN ON TOP OF ME, BECAUSE AFTER THE DEATH OF MY MOTHER THAT HOUSE WAS NO LONGER A HOME—IT WAS JUST A HOUSE."

BONO
U2

PRINCE

"IT'S REAL HARD FOR MY FATHER TO SHOW EMOTION. HE NEVER SAYS 'I LOVE YOU,' AND WHENEVER WE TRY TO HUG OR SOMETHING, WE BANG OUR HEADS TOGETHER LIKE IN SOME CHARLIE CHAPLIN MOVIE. BUT A WHILE AGO, HE WAS TELLING ME HOW I ALWAYS HAD TO BE CAREFUL. MY FATHER TOLD ME, 'IF ANYTHING HAPPENS TO YOU, I'M GONE.' ALL I THOUGHT AT FIRST WAS THAT IT WAS A REAL NICE THING TO SAY. BUT THEN I THOUGHT ABOUT IT FOR A WHILE AND REALIZED SOMETHING. THAT WAS MY FATHER'S WAY OF SAYING 'I LOVE YOU.'"

Rolling Stone, September 12, 1985

FAMILY AND FRIENDSHIP

JOE STRUMMER
THE CLASH

"...I SHUDDER TO THINK WHAT WOULD HAVE HAPPENED IF I HADN'T GONE TO BOARDING SCHOOL. I ONLY SAW MY FATHER TWICE A YEAR. IF I'D SEEN HIM ALL THE TIME I'D PROBABLY HAVE MURDERED HIM BY NOW."

Melody Maker, November 13, 1976

"MY FATHER WAS A STRANGER TO ME, AND I LEARNED THAT MY STEPFATHER WAS FIGHTING A LOSING BATTLE WITH MY MOTHER. ALMOST EVERYONE IS UNHAPPY WITH THEMSELVES WHEN THEY REALIZE WHAT THEY'VE DONE. AND THE LOT OF THEM GET MARRIED BECAUSE OF THE KIDS AND THAT'S A REALLY BAD IDEA. PEOPLE JUST RIP EACH OTHER TO SHREDS OVER THE YEARS. NOTHING KILLS A RELATIONSHIP LIKE COMMITMENT."

**LEMMY
MOTÖRHEAD**

Spin, October 19, 2012

FAMILY AND FRIENDSHIP

"…MY FATHER WAS THE BEST MAN IN THE WORLD AND PROBABLY WORTH A HUNDRED OF ME, BUT HE DIDN'T UNDERSTAND ME. THE TOWN HE LIVED IN AND THE TOWN I LIVED IN WERE NOT THE SAME."

BOB DYLAN

Chronicles: Volume One,
Simon & Schuster, 2004

Interview magazine, June 1978

"OH, I HAVE A VERY STRONG PATERNAL STREAK. I'M A BORN FATHER...I GET SUCH ENJOYMENT OUT OF BEING WITH CHILDREN. NOW THEY ARE ENJOYABLE LITTLE THINGS. THEY REALLY ARE. I LIKE THEIR KIND OF HUMOR. YOU CAN STUFF ALL YOUR PUNK BANDS, GIVE ME THREE CHILDREN INSTEAD."

DAVID BOWIE

FAMILY AND FRIENDSHIP

I'm a Believer: My Life of Monkees,
Music and Madness, Hyperion 1993

"MY MOM WAS A REAL MOM'S MOM. THREE SQUARE MEALS A DAY, WHETHER YOU WANTED THEM OR NOT. FLOORS SO CLEAN YOU COULD EAT OFF THEM. I USED TO GET UP AT NIGHT TO PEE AND SHE WOULD MAKE THE BED."

MICKY DOLENZ
THE MONKEES

PAUL SIMON

"THE THING ABOUT MY MOTHER WAS THAT SHE WAS EXTREMELY SUPPORTIVE. NOT THAT MY FATHER WASN'T, BUT MY MOTHER WAS THE FIRST NOURISHING PERSON IN MY LIFE. SHE MADE ME FEEL AS IF I COULD TAKE MY NEEDS VERY SERIOUSLY, BECAUSE SHE DID."

Playboy, February 1984

FAMILY AND FRIENDSHIP

JOHN LYDON

"IT WAS HARD TRYING TO BE THE REBELLIOUS ONE HERE IN YOUR ROOM WHEN YOUR MUM'S SITTING THERE LISTENING TO *FUN HOUSE*. OH NO! GET ME OUT OF THIS CRAZY FAMILY!"

Rotten: No Irish No Blacks No Dogs,
St. Martin's Press, 1993

"I'M A BAD SON. I DON'T CALL HER ENOUGH. SHE'LL JUST KEEP ME ON THE PHONE AND TELL ME THAT SHE LOVES ME. AND I'LL BE LIKE, 'YEAH, YEAH, YEAH. MOM, I GOTTA GO.' THE LAST THING YOU WANT TO DO WHEN YOU'RE HOME AFTER A TOUR AND YOUR GIRLFRIEND'S OVER IS CALL YOUR MOM."

ALBERT HAMMOND, JR.
THE STROKES

Rolling Stone, November 12, 2003

FAMILY AND FRIENDSHIP

"MOM DIDN'T DISCIPLINE US MUCH, EXCEPT TO WARN US THAT OUR DAD MIGHT. IF WE WERE DOING SOMETHING BAD, SHE WOULD STAND BACK A LITTLE BIT AND PUT UP A FINGER. 'YOU'D BETTER WATCH OUT,' SHE'D SAY, 'OR YOUR DAD IS GOING TO GET YOU.' SHE WAS RIGHT ABOUT THAT. MY DAD WAS DIFFERENT FROM MY MOM. IF HE WANTED US TO WAKE UP, HE WOULD STAND IN THE DOOR OF THE BEDROOM AND SAY, 'HEY! GET UP!' EVEN WHEN HE WAS SPEAKING SOFTLY, HIS VOICE WASN'T SOFT."

BRIAN WILSON
THE BEACH BOYS

I Am Brian Wilson: A Memoir,
Da Capo Press, 2016

Twitter, August 3, 2012

"ACCORDING TO MY RESEARCH DUDES WHO DO REALLY EMBARRASSING AIR GUITAR MAKE GREAT DADS."

NEKO CASE

FAMILY AND FRIENDSHIP

*The Playboy Interviews with John Lennon
and Yoko Ono*, Playboy Press, 1981

"SO THE JOY IS STILL THERE WHEN I SEE SEAN. HE DIDN'T COME OUT OF MY BELLY BUT, BY GOD, I MADE HIS BONES, BECAUSE I'VE ATTENDED TO EVERY MEAL, AND TO HOW HE SLEEPS, AND TO THE FACT THAT HE SWIMS LIKE A FISH. THAT'S BECAUSE I TOOK HIM TO THE 'Y.' I TOOK HIM TO THE OCEAN. I'M SO PROUD OF THOSE THINGS. HE IS MY BIGGEST PRIDE, YOU SEE."

JOHN LENNON
THE BEATLES

JARVIS COCKER
PULP

"ONE DAY I'D LIKE TO HAVE CHILDREN. IT SEEMS UNNATURAL NOT TO, BUT I WORRY SOMETIMES THAT I'M GETTING A BIT LONG IN THE TOOTH. YOU KNOW, IT MIGHT BE HANDY TO BE AROUND TO WATCH THEM GROW UP, RATHER THAN SHOOT YOUR LOAD AND THEN DIE."

Mojo, November 2001

FAMILY AND FRIENDSHIP

NOEL GALLAGHER
OASIS

"HE'S RUDE, ARROGANT, INTIMIDATING AND LAZY. HE'S THE ANGRIEST MAN YOU'LL EVER MEET. HE'S LIKE A MAN WITH A FORK IN A WORLD OF SOUP."

on his brother Liam, *Q*, April 2009

"I LIVE IN A HOUSE-LOAD OF WOMEN, WHICH SOME-TIMES CAN DRIVE ME TOTALLY ROUND THE BEND, WHICH IS WHY I NEED TO WORK AND GET ON THE ROAD. I LOVE 'EM ALL, BUT IT'S WEIRD TO BE LIVING WITH A LOAD OF CHICKS—IT DOESN'T MATTER WHAT AGE THEY ARE. FOR A GUY, THE ONLY GUY IN THE HOUSE, YOU GOTTA CALL UP ANOTHER CAT AND SAY, 'HEY, COME OVER, OR I'LL JUST DROP OVER THERE!'"

KEITH RICHARDS
THE ROLLING STONES

Rolling Stone, October 6, 1988

FAMILY AND FRIENDSHIP

"I PRIDE MYSELF ON LOYALTY TO EVERYONE, FROM THE PEOPLE IN THE ROAD CREW TO MY FAMILY. THAT'S A BIG PART OF MY LIFE: KEEPING THOSE RELATIONSHIPS INTACT."

DAVE GROHL
FOO FIGHTERS

Brisbane Times, October 6, 2007

The Quietus, April 27, 2015

"THERE'S NOTHING WORSE THAN FALLING OUT WITH PEOPLE AND NOT RESOLVING THAT."

DAMON ALBARN
BLUR

FAMILY AND FRIENDSHIP

160

Rolling Stone, November 29, 1979

"I THANK GOD I HAVE ENOUGH CLOSE FRIENDS WHO WOULD TELL ME IF I WERE MESSING UP MY LIFE. THANK GOD FOR THE LOVE AND SUPPORT I'VE RECEIVED FROM THEM. BUT IF THERE'S A NIGHT TO PARTY, LIKE TONIGHT, YOU GO RIGHT AFUCKINHEAD."

GLENN FREY
EAGLES

SIOUXSIE SIOUX
SIOUXSIE & THE BANSHEES

"I DON'T HAVE ANY FRIENDS FROM BEFORE. I HAVEN'T GOT ANY SCHOOL CHUMS. I DIDN'T HAVE ANY DEEP FRIENDSHIPS IN SCHOOL BECAUSE IT WAS SILLY GIRLS TALKING ABOUT THEIR BOYFRIENDS. I THOUGHT THEY WERE ALL A BIT RIDICULOUS SO I TENDED TO HANG OUT QUITE A LOT WITH MY OLDER BROTHER AND SISTER."

Smash Hits,
November 22-December 5, 1984

FAMILY AND FRIENDSHIP

PAUL SIMONON
THE CLASH

"FRIENDS TURN AGAINST YOU QUICKER THAN ANYONE. LIKE AT SCHOOL, IT'S ALWAYS YOUR BEST MATES THAT TURN AGAINST YOU. YOU DON'T THINK ANYTHING OF IT. YOU JUST HAVE TO TURN THE OTHER WAY AND GET ON WITH WHAT YOU'RE DOING."

Melody Maker, November 25, 1978

"I'VE ALWAYS LAID MY PLANS VERY SECRE-
TIVELY AND NOT LET ANYONE IN ON THEM,
WHICH MORE OFTEN THAN NOT HAS TURNED
OUT TO BE A MISTAKE. I DIDN'T KNOW THAT IT
WAS POSSIBLE TO TALK THINGS OVER WITH
PEOPLE AND NOT LOSE EVERYTHING IN THE
PROCESS. I THOUGHT THE MINUTE YOU CON-
FIDED ANYTHING IT WOULD DISAPPEAR."

MARIANNE FAITHFULL

Faithfull: An Autobiography,
Cooper Square Press, 1994

FAMILY AND FRIENDSHIP

164

"WELL, MOST OF MY FRIENDS ARE IN MEM-
PHIS. THAT'S WHY I ESTABLISHED A HOME
THERE. WE'VE BEEN KICKED OUT OF THE
SAME PLACES, YOU KNOW, IT'S EASIER TO
BE YOURSELF THERE."

ELVIS
PRESLEY

DIG magazine, 1957

FIVE GREAT
ROCK & ROLL
Memoirs

1. BOB DYLAN, *CHRONICLES: VOLUME ONE* (2004)—Dylan's fragmentary autobiography is like the best of his songwriting: powerful, challenging, and defiant. A fascinating insight into the creative mind of one of the real titans of American music.

2. PATTI SMITH, *JUST KIDS* (2010)—Ostensibly a self-portrait of the emerging young artist with her companion Robert Mapplethorpe, it is a vivid depiction of the underground cultural landscape that would define New York for multiple generations.

3. KEITH RICHARDS, *LIFE* (2010)—A richly detailed account from the Rolling Stone that offers a candid and entertaining look back at the adventures, the gigs, the drugs, his bandmates, and his gift for survival.

4. KIM GORDON, *GIRL IN A BAND: A MEMOIR* (2015)—A remarkably poignant look at Gordon's personal and creative life, from her girlhood in California to the travails of marriage to Sonic Youth bandmate Thurston Moore, to motherhood, including a song-by-song examination of some of her most memorable work.

5. BRUCE SPRINGSTEEN, *BORN TO RUN* (2015)—As deeply affecting as any of his albums, *Born to Run* tells the evocative story of his upbringing, as well as the personal and professional struggles that define him as a musician and as a man. Especially notable for describing his battle with depression and the effort to reach an understanding with his father.

chapter six
GROWING UP
and Growing Old

Time stops for no one, and whether you're inclined to look back or look ahead, growing up and growing old can come with new insights or outlooks on life. "Never trust anyone over thirty" was the hippie maxim, at least until all the hippies hit the magic number and kept on growing old. Some rock stars, regardless of their age, refuse to grow up, while others have always seemed wise beyond their years.

The Rock & Roll Wisdom Playlist

Bruce Springsteen—"Growin' Up"
David Bowie—"Changes"
Fleetwood Mac—"Landslide"
Pulp—"Disco 2000"
LCD Soundsystem—"Losing My Edge"

Hy Gardner Calling, 1956

"I WAS RAISED IN A PRETTY DECENT HOME AND EVERYTHING. MY FOLKS ALWAYS MADE ME BEHAVE WHETHER I WANTED TO OR NOT."

ELVIS PRESLEY

GROWING UP AND GROWING OLD

I Dreamed I Was a Very Clean Tramp:
An Autobiography, Ecco, 2013

"I GREW UP THINKING MEN WORKED BEST IN WANDERING SMALL TEAMS, USUALLY TWO-MAN. YOU NEEDED SOMEONE TO CONSPIRE WITH, SOME TO HELP YOU MAINTAIN THE NERVE TO CARRY OUT YOUR IDEAS. SOMEONE TO KNOW WHAT YOU WERE THINKING (OTHERWISE YOUR THINKING DIDN'T REALLY EXIST). SOMEONE WHO HAD QUALITIES YOU WANTED, MAYBE TOO, AND THAT YOU COULD ACQUIRE TO SOME DEGREE BY ASSOCIATION...I WANTED TO HAVE A LIFE OF ADVENTURE. I DIDN'T WANT ANYBODY TELLING ME WHAT TO DO. I KNEW THIS WAS THE MOST IMPORTANT THING AND THAT ALL WOULD BE LOST IF I PRETENDED OTHERWISE LIKE GROWN-UPS DID."

RICHARD HELL

JAMES BROWN

"MY ENVIRONMENT—THE SLUMS OF THE SOUTH—
CREATED ME, AND I IN TURN CREATED THE MUSIC THAT
THAT ENVIRONMENT CONNECTED ME TO. IT'S ALL A
GIANT CIRCLE OF LIFE, ENDLESS AND CONTINUOUS AS
THE SHAPE OF AN OLD VINYL RECORD OR A NEW CD."

I Feel Good, A Memoir of a Life in Soul,
New American Library, 2005

GROWING UP AND GROWNING OLD

TOM PETTY

"I DIDN'T GO [TO SCHOOL] A LOT. ONCE I GOT IN A BAND, HOW COULD I TAKE IT SERI-OUSLY? THIS GUY WORRYING ABOUT MY HAIR TOUCHING MY EARS IS GONNA TEACH ME SOMETHING? I FAILED EVERYTHING. NEVER DID NO HOMEWORK."

Creem, August 1978

"I GREW UP BEING TOLD BY PSYCHOTIC ADULTS THAT I WAS FILLED WITH SIN, THAT MY EXPERIENCES DIDN'T MATTER, AND THAT I WOULD DIE BEFORE I REACHED ADULTHOOD BECAUSE WE WERE LIVING IN THE END TIMES. I MADE A DECISION AS A CHILD THAT I WOULD NEVER LET ANYONE TELL ME THAT I WAS INVALID OR INAUTHENTIC, OR THAT MY EXPERIENCES WERE."

FATHER JOHN MISTY

Pitchfork, March 16, 2017

GROWING UP AND GROWING OLD

"MY CHILDHOOD WAS NOT ALL SUFFERING. IT WAS NOT ALL SLUM. I WAS ALWAYS *WELL* DRESSED, *WELL* FED, *WELL* SCHOOLED, AND BROUGHT UP TO BE A NICE LOWER-MIDDLE-CLASS ENGLISH BOY. AND THAT'S WHAT MADE THE BEATLES DIFFERENT, THE FACT THAT GEORGE, PAUL AND JOHN WERE *GRAMMAR* SCHOOL BOYS."

JOHN LENNON
THE BEATLES

The Playboy Interviews with John Lennon and Yoko Ono, Playboy Press, 1981

Shortlist, May 3, 2012

"ON MY MUM'S SIDE, MY FAMILY ARE ALL FARMERS AND ARE VERY DOWN-TO-EARTH, REGULAR, WORKING PEOPLE. WHEN I WAS A LITTLE KID, I ALWAYS THOUGHT I WAS GOING TO BE A FARMER, BELIEVE IT OR NOT. I WAS CONVINCED, AND THAT WAS ALL I WANTED TO BE. UNTIL ABOUT THE AGE OF 11 OR 12— AND THEN I BECAME GRIPPED BY MUSIC."

DAMON ALBARN
BLUR

GROWING UP AND GROWNING OLD

Rolling Stone, May 28, 1970

"KIDS ARE LEAVING HOME BECAUSE THEY CAN'T TALK TO THEIR MOTHERS, THEY'D RATHER TALK TO A FRIEND; YOUNG FELLAS CAN'T TALK TO THEIR FATHERS, BECAUSE THEIR PARENTS THINK THEY'RE CRAZY. BUT THEY'RE NOT CRAZY, THEY'RE JUST WISE AND THEY'VE GOT MORE NERVE TO DO WHAT THEY WANTED TO DO AND COULDN'T DO. THEY'RE THE REAL FOLK THAT THE PHONIES DON'T WANT THE WORLD TO KNOW THEY'RE REAL."

LITTLE RICHARD

JAVIS COCKER
PULP

"MAYBE IT'S COS I'M IMMATURE, BUT ADOLESCENCE INTERESTS ME BECAUSE IT'S SUCH AN EMOTIONALLY CHARGED TIME. YOU'VE NOT DONE IT YET, ALL THAT MUCH, AND YOU'RE TAKING THIS AMAZING STEP. IT'S ALWAYS ON YOUR MIND. KIDS AREN'T PC ABOUT IT, EITHER. THEY'LL GO OUT WITH SOMEONE FOR TWO WEEKS AND THEN PACK 'EM IN, BUT IT DOESN'T END UP IN THE DIVORCE COURTS. YOU FEEL CRAP FOR A FEW DAYS, THEN FIND SOMEONE ELSE. PEOPLE GET MORE FURTIVE AND PERVERSE AS THEY GET OLDER. I'M HOPING TO EXTEND MY ADOLESCENCE AS FAR AS POSSIBLE."

Vox, May 1995

GROWING UP AND GROWNING OLD

MORRISSEY
THE SMITHS

"I WAS NEVER HAPPY WHEN I WAS YOUNG SO I DON'T EQUATE GROWING UP WITH BEING HYSTERICALLY UNHAPPY. TO ME OLD AGE DOESN'T MEAN DOOM, DESPAIR AND DEFEAT. THERE ARE LOTS OF PEOPLE I KNOW IN CONSIDERABLY ADVANCED YEARS THAT I FIND FASCINATING."

Smash Hits Yearbook 1985

"I'M LESS CONFUSED AND MORE WILLING TO ACCEPT THINGS. MAYBE IT'S JUST BECAUSE I GOT OLDER. IT TAKES TIME TO PUT YOURSELF AND YOUR ACHIEVEMENTS INTO SOME KIND OF PERSPECTIVE AND TO UNDERSTAND WHAT THERE IS TO VALUE IN LIFE. I'VE TRIED HARD AND I'VE HAD MORE SUCCESS THAN MOST PEOPLE AND I'M HAPPY. IT SHOULD BE ENOUGH."

PAUL SIMON

Rolling Stone, May 28, 1970

GROWING UP AND GROWNING OLD

"I REALLY CAN'T BELIEVE IT'S THIRTY YEARS SINCE THE '60S. I FIND IT STAGGERING. IT'S LIKE THE FUTURE, THE '60S TO ME, IT'S LIKE IT HASN'T HAPPENED. I FEEL THE '60S ARE ABOUT TO ARRIVE. AND WE'RE IN SOME SORT OF TIME WARP AND IT'S STILL GOING TO HAPPEN."

Paul McCartney: Many Years From Now,
Secker & Warburg, 1997

Company, 1988

"IT'S NOT GROWING OLDER THAT FRIGHTENS ME; IT'S THE IDEA OF GETTING STUCK IN A RUT, OF BECOMING NARROW-MINDED AND UNHAPPY. I'D HATE TO GET TO A POINT WHERE I REALIZED THAT I'D ALREADY LIVED THE MOST ENJOYABLE AND INTERESTING PART OF MY LIFE AND THAT IT WAS GOING TO BE BORING FROM NOW ON. NOTHING WORRIES ME MORE THAN BOREDOM, OR WASTING TIME. WE'VE LIVED VERY FAST."

SIMON LE BON
DURAN DURAN

GROWING UP AND GROWING OLD

182

Rolling Stone, November 29, 1979

"YA KNOW, THE GREAT THING ABOUT BEING THIRTY IS THERE ARE SO MANY MORE AVAILABLE WOMEN. THE YOUNG ONES LOOK YOUNGER AND THE OLD ONES DON'T LOOK NEARLY AS OLD."

GLENN FREY
EAGLES

SHIRLEY MANSON
GARBAGE

"I LOOK AT ALL MY HEROINES LIKE DEBBIE HARRY AND CHRISSIE HYNDE AND ALL OF THEM WERE LATE START-ERS. DEBBIE HARRY WAS 29 OR WHATEVER WHEN SHE HAD HER FIRST HIT; CHRISSIE HYNDE WAS 28. I REALLY THINK THAT'S IN OUR FAVOR. OUR COLLECTIVE EXPERIENCE HAS ALLOWED US A FREEDOM THAT VERY FEW BANDS HAVE. WHEN YOU GET OLDER YOU CAN'T RELY ON THE FIRE IN YOUR BELLY ANYMORE AND YOU HAVE TO LEARN TO PILOT YOUR OWN PLANE. WE PILOT OUR OWN PLANE."

NME, March 21, 1998

GROWING UP AND GROWNING OLD

184

JOHN LENNON
THE BEATLES

"I AM GOING TO BE FORTY, AND LIFE BEGINS AT FORTY, SO THEY PROMISE. OH, I *BELIEVE* IT, TOO. BECAUSE I FEEL FINE. I'M, LIKE, *EXCITED.* IT'S LIKE TWENTY-ONE—YOU KNOW, HITTING TWENTY-ONE. IT'S LIKE: *WOW!* WHAT'S GOING TO HAPPEN NEXT?"

The Playboy Interviews with John Lennon and Yoko Ono, Playboy Press, 1981

185

"THE IRONY IS THAT NOW THAT I ACTUALLY AM IN MIDLIFE, NOW THAT I'M A FULLY-FLEDGED MIDDLE AGE MAN, I DON'T FEEL LIKE I'M HAVING A MIDLIFE CRISIS ANYMORE. THAT SAID, I AM VERY AWARE OF THE ABSURDITY OF BEING A 51-YEAR-OLD MUSICIAN IN 2016. NONE OF THIS IS WHAT I EVER EXPECTED. I KNOW THAT SOME MUSICIANS WHEN THEY RELEASE AN ALBUM, THEY TRY REALLY HARD TO PRETEND THAT THEY'RE 10 OR 20 YEARS YOUNGER AND THAT THEIR CAREER IS WHAT IT USED TO BE. I ACTUALLY FIND IT QUITE LIBERATING TO BE 51 YEARS OLD MAKING ALBUMS AT A TIME WHEN PEOPLE DON'T REALLY PAY THAT MUCH ATTENTION TO ALBUMS."

MOBY

The Talks, *New York Times*,
December 14, 2016

GROWING UP AND GROWNING OLD

"YOU LOOK AT YOURSELF WHEN YOU'RE YOUNG AND YOU THINK, WHY COULDN'T YOU HAVE BEEN A BLOODY BIT SMARTER? OF COURSE YOU CAN'T. I'M DESPONDENT ABOUT THE EARLY YEARS OF MY YOUTH. I WAS TERRIFIED BY EVERYTHING, SUCH A LITTLE PUSSY, REALLY."

JOHN LYDON

Rotten: No Irish, No Blacks, No Dogs,
St. Martin's Press, 1993

Girl in a Band: A Memoir,
Dey Street Books, 2015

"THE IMAGE A LOT OF PEOPLE HAVE OF ME AS DETACHED, IMPAS-SIVE, OR REMOTE IS A PERSONA THAT COMES FROM YEARS OF BEING TEASED FOR EVERY FEELING I EVER EXPRESSED. WHEN I WAS YOUNG, THERE WAS NEVER ANY SPACE FOR ME TO GET ATTENTION OF MY OWN THAT WASN'T NEGATIVE. ART, AND THE PRACTICE OF MAKING ART, WAS THE ONLY SPACE THAT WAS MINE ALONE, WHERE I COULD BE ANYONE AND DO ANYTHING, WHERE JUST BY USING MY HEAD AND MY HANDS I COULD CRY, OR LAUGH, OR GET PISSED OFF."

KIM GORDON
SONIC YOUTH

GROWING UP AND GROWNING OLD

Unfaithful Music & Disappearing Ink,
Blue Rider Press, 2015

"LIFE TAKES MUCH LONGER THAN THE AVERAGE POP SONG. IT IS FULL OF WRONG CHOICES AND INCONVENIENT ABANDONED RESPONSIBILITIES. IT IS MUCH MORE PAINFUL AND LESS EASILY FORGIVEN."

ELVIS COSTELLO

NOEL GALLAGHER
OASIS

"I'M PROUD OF THREE THINGS, MAYBE FOUR THINGS. TO GET TO THIS AGE AND NOT HAVE DYED MY HAIR IS A MAJOR ACHIEVEMENT. NO EARRINGS. NO TATTOOS. AND NO MOTORBIKE."

Esquire UK, November 5, 2015

GROWING UP AND GROWING OLD

MICK JAGGER
THE ROLLING STONES

"I'VE WORKED OUT THAT I'D BE 50 IN 1984. I'D BE DEAD! HORRIBLE, ISN'T IT. HALFWAY TO A HUNDRED. UGH! I CAN SEE MYSELF COMING ONSTAGE IN MY BLACK, WINDOWED INVALID CARRIAGE WITH A STICK. THEN I TURN ROUND, WIGGLE MY BOTTOM AT THE AUDIENCE, AND SAY SOMETHING LIKE 'NOW HERE'S AN OLD SONG YOU MIGHT REMEMBER CALLED SATISFACTION.'"

Disc, May 21, 1966

"I KNOW A FEW GROOVY MIDDLE-AGED PEOPLE, BUT NOT MANY."

KEITH RICHARDS
THE ROLLING STONES

Sunday People, October 9, 1966

GROWING UP AND GROWNING OLD

192

"SOMETIMES I THINK I AM AN ADULT AND THEN I REMEMBER I HAD AN ICE CREAM CONE FOR DINNER."

ST. VINCENT

Twitter, August 30, 2012

LIVE FAST, DIE YOUNG:
THIRTY ROCK STARS WHO NEVER
Made it to Thirty

BUDDY HOLLY, 22 years old: Died in a plane crash February 3, 1959, alongside fellow musicians **RITCHIE VALENS**, 17, and **JILES PERRY RICHARDSON, JR., A.K.A., THE BIG BOPPER**, 28.

EDDIE COCHRAN: Died in an automobile accident on April 16, 1960, at the age of 21.

STUART SUTCLIFFE, the Beatles: Died of a brain hemorrhage at the age of 21 on April 10, 1962.

RUDY LEWIS, the Drifters: Though no autopsy was performed, authorities listed his cause of death at the age of 27 on May 21, 1964, as a possible drug overdose.

BOBBY FULLER: Found dead at the age of 23 in a car outside his Los Angeles apartment on July 18, 1966, the circumstances of his death are still a mystery.

FRANKIE LYMON: Died of a heroin overdose on February 27, 1968. He was 25 years old.

BRIAN JONES: Discovered lying motionless at the bottom of his swimming pool on July 3, 1969. He was 27 years old, and the coroner's report stated it was "death by misadventure."

JIMI HENDRIX: Died of asphyxiation on September 18, 1970, at the age of 27.

JANIS JOPLIN: Died of a heroin overdose on October 4, 1970. She was 27 years old.

DUANE ALLMAN: Died at 24 in a motorcycle crash on October 29, 1971.

RON "PIGPEN" MCKERNAN, Grateful Dead: Died of a gastrointestinal hemorrhage on March 8, 1973, at the age of 27.

GRAM PARSONS, the Flying Burrito Brothers: Died of an overdose of morphine and alcohol on September 19, 1973. He was 26 years old.

PETE HAM, Badfinger: Committed suicide by hanging himself on April 24, 1975, at the age of 27.

MARC BOLAN, T. Rex: Died in a car accident two weeks shy of his 30th birthday on September 16, 1977.

CHRIS BELL, Big Star: Died on December 27, 1978, in a car accident. He was 27 years old.

SID VICIOUS, Sex Pistols: Died of a drug overdose on February 2, 1979, at the age of 21.

IAN CURTIS, Joy Division: Committed suicide by hanging himself on May 18, 1980. He was 23 years old.

DARBY CRASH, Germs: Died of suicide by heroin overdose on December 7, 1980, at the age of 22.

RANDY RHOADS: Died in a plane crash at 25 years old on March 19, 1982.

NICHOLAS DINGLEY, A.K.A. RAZZLE, Hanoi Rocks: Died in an automobile accident on December 8, 1984, at the age of 24. Vince Neil of Mötley Crüe was the driver of the car.

D. BOON, Minutemen: Died in a van accident at the age of 27 on December 22, 1985.

CLIFF BURTON, Metallica: Died in a tour bus accident on September 27, 1986. He was 24 years old.

HILLEL SLOVAK, Red Hot Chili Peppers: Died of a heroin overdose at the age of 26 on June 25, 1988.

PETE DE FREITAS, Echo & the Bunnymen: Died in a motorcycle accident on June 14, 1989, at the age of 27.

ANDREW WOOD, Mother Love Bone: Died on March 19, 1990, three days after a heroin overdose and hemorrhage aneurysm. He was 24 years old.

KURT COBAIN, Nirvana: Died of a self-inflicted gun shot at the age of 27 on April 5, 1994.

RICHEY EDWARDS, Manic Street Preachers: Disappeared on February 1, 1995, and though his whereabouts are still unknown he was only declared presumed dead in 2008. He was 27 years old at the time of his disappearance.

SHANNON HOON, Blind Melon: Died of a cocaine overdose on October 21, 1995, at the age of 28.

chapter seven
DEBAUCHERY
and Excess

Though not all rock stars dabble in drugs, drown themselves in booze, or lead lives on the wrong side of the law, enough of them have done so—and done so famously—that the genre has something of a well-earned reputation for sordid behavior under the influence.

The Rock & Roll Wisdom Playlist

The Velvet Underground—"Heroin"
The Doors—"Alabama Song (Whisky Bar)"
Oasis—"Cigarettes & Alcohol"
Ramones—"Now I Wanna Sniff Some Glue"
Motörhead—"White Line Fever"

"DRUGS AND ALCOHOL CHANGES THINGS. IT CHANGES HOW YOU WORK, THE HOURS YOU WORK. THAT WAS THE PROBLEM. YOU'D WORK STRAIGHT FOR THREE DAYS AND THEN SLEEP FOR TWO."

CHARLIE WATTS
THE ROLLING STONES

Mojo, January 2012

DEBAUCHERY AND EXCESS

"ON A VERY BASIC LEVEL, I LOVE DRINKING. BUT I CAN'T SEE DRINKING JUST MILK OR WATER OR COCA COLA. IT JUST RUINS IT FOR ME. YOU HAVE TO HAVE WINE OR BEER TO COMPLETE A MEAL."

JIM MORRISON
THE DOORS

Rolling Stone, July 26, 1969

The Talks, *New York Times*,
December 12, 2013

"EVERYBODY LIKES TO WATCH A DRUNK GORILLA SMASH SHIT."

MATT BERNINGER
THE NATIONAL

DEBAUCHERY AND EXCESS

The Ottawa Journal, April 18, 1969

"I DRINK TO RELAX AND TO KIND OF TURN MYSELF INSIDE OUT AND JUST LET MYSELF GO."

JANIS JOPLIN

203

FRANK ZAPPA

"I HAVE SMOKED MARIJUANA. SMOKED MARIJUANA TEN TIMES. MADE ME SLEEPY AND GAVE ME A SORE THROAT. I CAN'T UNDERSTAND WHY ANYBODY WOULD WANT TO DEVOTE THEIR LIFE TO A CAUSE LIKE DOPE. THAT'S THE MOST BORING PASTIME I CAN THING OF. IT RANKS A CLOSE SECOND TO TELEVISION."

Creem, January 1976

DEBAUCHERY AND EXCESS

MICK JAGGER
THE ROLLING STONES

"IT'S REALLY DIFFICULT TO GET OUT OF THE GOSSIP COLUMNS ONCE YOU'VE GOTTEN IN. SURE, I'D LIKE TO SEE A CHANGE. I DON'T REALLY LIKE BEING IN GOSSIP COLUMNS. IT'S NOT REALLY WHAT I LIKE DOING. BUT IT'S BEEN LIKE THAT FOR SO LONG. IT'S NO NEW THING. I'VE BEEN IN GOSSIP COLUMNS SINCE '63-'64. IT'S LIKE A SOAP OPERA THAT KEEPS GOING ON AND ON AND ON."

Creem, January 1978

"MY BUST REALLY SORT OF BROUGHT THINGS TO A HEAD. IT'S SUCH A FUNNY STORY. YOU COULDN'T MAKE IT UP AS FICTION, REALLY. YOU CAN'T ARREST SOMEBODY IF THEY'RE NOT AWAKE, AND I'D BEEN UP FOR FOUR OR FIVE DAYS AND I'D JUST GONE TO SLEEP AND THEN THE MOUNTIES ARRIVED. THEY'RE WALKING ME AROUND THE ROOM APPARENTLY—I MEAN, THIS IS THE STORY I HEAR 'COS I'M ASLEEP, SO I'M WALKING AROUND THE ROOM, THERE WERE TWO MOUNTIES, UNTIL I FINALLY SORT OF SNAPPED-TO ENOUGH FOR THEM TO SAY, 'OK, HE'S ALL RIGHT, YOU'RE UNDER ARREST.' OH GREAT! I PROMPTLY GO BACK TO SLEEP AGAIN. I WAS KNACKERED."

KEITH RICHARDS
THE ROLLING STONES

Uncut, December 2002

DEBAUCHERY AND EXCESS

"A LIGHT BULB WENT ON IN MY HEAD WHEN I READ *NAKED LUNCH.* I REALIZED, ANY TIME YOU WANT TO ESCAPE THIS WORLD, THIS IS WHAT YOU DO: YOU GO OUT AND BECOME A JUNKIE AND LIVE ON THE STREET. OF COURSE WHAT I DID NOT KNOW WAS THAT YOU CAN'T PLAY AROUND WITH HEROIN. HEROIN IS AS CLOSE AS YOU'LL EVER GET TO DEATH WHILE YOU'RE STILL LIVING."

MARIANNE FAITHFULL

Memories, Dreams and Reflections,
Fourth Estate, 2007

Interview by Howard Smith, March 1969.
From *The Smith Tapes: Lost Interviews with
Rock Stars & Icons 1969–1972*,
Princeton Architectural Press, 2015

"I'M SAYING IT'S A POOR WAY TO BORE YOURSELF. THERE ARE BETTER WAYS OF BORING YOURSELF THAN DOPE...I'M INCLUDING POT AND LIQUOR. I SAY ANYTHING, *ANYTHING* THAT DISORIENTS YOU OR DISTRACTS YOU—ANYBODY TELLS YOU YOU'RE GETTIN' CLOSER TO REALITY IS LYING. THEY'RE PEOPLE WHO AREN'T VERY STRONG, THAT'S ALL."

LOU REED
THE VELVET UNDERGROUND

DEBAUCHERY AND EXCESS

Telling Stories, Penguin Viking, 2012

"I PASSED OUT ONCE IN A BIN-LINER, AND WHEN I CAME ROUND THE GLUE HAD DRIED AND I HAD IT STUCK IN MY HAIR; NOT JUST A FEW STRANDS, BUT ALL OF MY HAIR."

TIM BURGESS
THE CHARLATANS

STERLING MORRISON
THE VELVET UNDERGROUND

"THEY USED TO GIVE THORAZINE TO DANGEROUS PSYCHOTICS—IT DEFINITELY SUBDUES YOU. IT PUTS YOU IN KIND OF A CATATONIC-LIKE STATE, HA HA HA. I'D WASH IT DOWN WITH ALCOHOL AND SEE IF I WAS ALIVE THE NEXT MORNING."

Please Kill Me: The Uncensored Oral History of Punk, Grove Press, 1996

DEBAUCHERY AND EXCESS

MICK JAGGER
THE ROLLING STONES

"I DON'T REGRET ANYTHING AND I AM VERY FOND OF ALL OF IT. MY YEARS WITH THE ROLLING STONES ARE AND WERE A WONDERFUL TIME, REALLY. I MEAN, YOU COULD PAINT IT IN A VERY DARK LIGHT: IT WAS DECADENT, YEAH IT WAS QUITE DECADENT, BUT DECADENCE IS VERY ENJOYABLE, ISN'T IT?"

The Talks, *New York Times*, June 22, 2011

"AT TIMES WHEN I WAS HEAVILY DOPED I NEVER GOT ANY CHICKS. AT TIMES WHEN I WAS PLAYING GOOD I NEVER GOT ANY CHICKS—OR ANY DOPE. YOU REALLY CAN'T HAVE ALL THREE AT ONCE UNLESS YOU'RE A PHYSICAL DYNAMO."

PETE TOWNSHEND
THE WHO

Creem, January 1974

DEBAUCHERY AND EXCESS

"I'VE WOKEN UP MORE TIMES IN JAIL THAN I HAVE IN HOTELS. MIND YOU, I'M NOT COMPLAINING BECAUSE THE FOOD'S BETTER."

Smash Hits, October 11-24, 1984

Kerrang!, July 1995

"PROBABLY THE MOST STUPID EXPENSIVE THING WAS JUST RECENTLY I BOUGHT TWO ALBINO BOA CONSTRICTORS, A MALE AND A FEMALE, FOR AN IMPRESSIVE AMOUNT OF MONEY. EVERYONE'S LIKE, YOU SPENT WHAT ON WHAT?"

SLASH
GUNS N' ROSES

DEBAUCHERY AND EXCESS

TOM PETTY

"I NEVER HAD A CAR WORTH A SHIT IN MY LIFE. SO I WENT OUT TO THE LOT AND SAID 'I WANNA HEAR ALL THE RADIOS.' I WENT THROUGH ALL THE CARS LISTENING TO THE STEREO AND THE TAPE DECK, AND WHEN I GOT THE BEST ONE I JUST PAID THE GUY CASH AND TOOK THE CAR. WHEN I LEFT, HE WAS STANDING THERE LOOKING DUMBFOUNDED, SO THAT WAS A GIGGLE. I WAS BROKE THE NEXT DAY."

Creem, August 1978

DEBAUCHERY AND EXCESS

NOEL GALLAGHER
OASIS

"I HAD BUILT FOR ME A CUSTOMIZED 1967 MARK II JAGUAR CONVERTIBLE AT A COST OF £110,000, AND I HAVEN'T GOT A DRIVING LICENSE. IT'S USELESS TO ME."

Blender, August 2008

BEST
ROCK & ROLL
Riders

1. VAN HALEN—Perhaps the most famous rider of all, Van Halen's extensive 1982 list included many fairly innocuous requests: Two cases of beer, meals for band and crew, one large tube of K-Y Jelly, etc. The line item which tipped the rider into legend was the demand for a bowl of M&Ms with all the brown ones removed. While many imagined some poor stagehand picking brown M&Ms out of bowls for hours because of an odd whim, many years later singer David Lee Roth revealed that it was a simple way of knowing immediately how closely a venue had read through the rider.

2. SLAYER—Thrash-metal legend Slayer made headlines with some of the requests in their rider for the 2011 iteration of Fun Fun Fun Fest in Austin, Texas. The unlikely list included four Lite-Brites, ten cases of Go-Gurt, a Hogan's Heroes DVD box set, 50,000 live bees, 100 snow-white goats for slaughter, sandwiches arranged as a pentagram, and a human skull full of Red Hots.

3. HAPPY MONDAYS—As known for their issues with excess as their shambolic sound, Madchester pioneers Happy

Mondays' rider once included a single bottle of absinthe, with the explicit caveat that it not be placed in the dressing room prior to showtime.

4. IGGY & THE STOOGES— Iggy Pop reunited with the Stooges in 2003, and along the way the group put together an extensive rider which included a humorous run through ordinarily dry technical requirements, along with specific needs for the dressing rooms. These included a Bob Hope impersonator, seven dwarves in Disney regalia, premium beer that "probably won't start with a letter 'B' and end with 'udweiser,'" and cauliflower and broccoli "cut into individual florets and immediately thrown in the garbage."

5. MARILYN MANSON—The shock rocker's requests may change from tour to tour, but one item appears to make the cut year after year: A bald, toothless hooker.

6. FOO FIGHTERS—Among the rock group's requests on their 2008 tour rider were a single bag of Pirate Booty; a range of breakfast cereals not left over from "last night's Dio show;" a collection of DVDs that don't feature Martin Lawrence, Jamie Kennedy, or sports; and a meal prepared for their roadies upon arrival so they're fueled up for their "arduous 70 to 90 minute work day."

chapter eight
MONEY
That's What I Want

I If Rock & Roll is all about defiance and rabble rousing, money shouldn't matter, or should it? The fact that so many of rock's biggest stars come from humble beginnings and have voracious ambitions creates yet another conflict.

The Rock & Roll Wisdom Playlist

Pink Floyd—"Money"
Cyndi Lauper—"Money Changes Everything"
Warren Zevon—"Lawyers, Guns, and Money"
Alice Cooper—"Billion Dollar Babies"
The Drifters—"Money Honey"

"I WAS TEARING AROUND MANHATTAN IN THE MIDDLE OF THE NIGHT WITH JIMMY DESTRI IN THIS BEATEN-UP OLD CAR, AND ASKING HIM WHY HE DIDN'T HAVE A HELICOPTER, AND HE WAS LIKE, 'BUY LAND!' I TOOK HIS ADVICE. I GOT MY FINANCIAL ADVICE FROM THE KEYBOARDIST IN BLONDIE AT THREE IN THE MORNING."

ALEX JAMES
BLUR

Q, June 2015

MONEY (THAT'S WHAT I WANT)

"WE'VE BEEN CRITICIZED BY ALL KINDS OF BANDS—WELL-MEANING BUT SHORT-SIGHTED, PEOPLE WITH SMALL DREAMS—'WHY DO YOU HAVE TO MAKE A MILLION DOLLARS A DAY? WHEN IS IT ENOUGH?' IT'S NEVER ENOUGH. IT'S ENDLESS."

GENE SIMMONS
KISS

Mojo, December 2009

Creem, March 1976

"SURE, I HAVE A MERCEDES BENZ AND A BEAUTIFUL HOME. I COULD AFFORD ALMOST ANYTHING. YES MA'AM, I'M A VERY WEALTHY MAN, BUT I'VE NEVER SEEN A BAND IN MY LIFE—THAT INCLUDES THE BEATLES—THAT IS WORTH WHAT THEY GET PAID. IT'S AMAZING AND RIDICULOUS HOW MUCH MONEY THEY GET PAID."

RONNIE VAN ZANT
LYNYRD SKYNYRD

MONEY (THAT'S WHAT I WANT)

Melody Maker, November 26, 1983

"THERE IS A LEVEL OF THE BUSINESS SIDE WHERE YOU'RE CONCERNED WITH MAKING MONEY, THE SAME AS ANY CAREER, YOU'RE CONCERNED TO KEEP IT COS IT'S YOUR LIVING. BUT THE DIFFERENCE IS THERE'S A BARRIER BETWEEN BEING CONCERNED ABOUT IT AND NOT ALLOWING IT TO TAKE OVER FROM THE ARTISTIC SIDE OF IT AND JUST BEING INFATUATED BY IT, LETTING IT CONTROL YOUR LIFE."

CURT SMITH
TEARS FOR FEARS

225

AL JARDINE
THE BEACH BOYS

"I'D RATHER BE STUPID, HAVE HAIR AND EARN MONEY."

NME, November 18, 1966

MONEY (THAT'S WHAT I WANT)

DENNIS WILSON
THE BEACH BOYS

"I STILL GIVE MY MONEY AWAY. I GIVE EVERYTHING I HAVE AWAY. WHAT I'M WEARING AND WHAT'S IN THAT CASE IS ALL I HAVE. I DON'T EVEN HAVE A CAR. I HAVE A 1934 DODGE PICKUP SOMEWHERE."

NME, June 28, 1969

"I WAS NEVER RICH, SO I HAVE VERY LITTLE REGARD FOR MONEY NOW. I ONLY RESPECT IT INASMUCH AS IT CAN FEED SOMEBODY. I GIVE A LOT OF THINGS AWAY, A LOT OF PRESENTS AND MONEY. MONEY IS BEST SPENT ON SOMEONE WHO NEEDS IT."

Rolling Stone, September 12, 1985

MONEY (THAT'S WHAT I WANT)

"LISTEN, I FELT LIKE A RICH MAN EVEN WHEN I HAD NO MONEY. I WOULD LIVE OFF MY GIRL-FRIEND'S POCKET MONEY OR THE PEOPLE ON THE STREET. MONEY HAS NEVER HAD ANYTHING TO DO WITH HOW RICH I FEEL. BUT IT IS ALMOST VILE FOR ME TO SAY THAT MONEY DOESN'T MEAN ANY-THING TO ME, BECAUSE IT MEANS A LOT TO MANY PEOPLE. IT MEANS A LOT IF YOU DON'T HAVE IT."

BONO
U2

Rolling Stone, October 8, 1987

Viva, March 1975

"I'VE DONE THE MONEY TRIP—THE LAST SORT OF GLORIOUS LIVING I DID WAS IN ASCOT HOUSE IN ENGLAND. IT WAS A BEAUTIFUL HOUSE AND VERY EXPENSIVE—TWO HUNDRED THOUSAND POUNDS, SUPPOSEDLY, ON SEVENTY-EIGHT ACRES. THAT WAS THE BIGGEST HOUSE I EVER HAD, AND BUYING IT WAS LIKE THE END OF THAT PARTICULAR DREAM. I STILL FOUND THAT I SPENT MOST OF THE TIME ON THE BED WITH THE TV OR IN THE RECORDING STUDIO. SO IT'S ALMOST THE SAME AS WHAT I'M DOING NOW, EXCEPT I CAN'T WALK OUT ONTO GRASS. YOU CAN PRETEND A LOT ON SEVENTY-EIGHT ACRES. I MEAN YOU CAN PRETEND YOU'RE ON THE MOON."

JOHN LENNON
THE BEATLES

MONEY (THAT'S WHAT I WANT)

Interview by Howard Smith, fall 1969.
From *The Smith Tapes: Lost Interviews with
Rock Stars & Icons 1969–1972*,
Princeton Architectural Press, 2015

"OH, YES, I CAN GO INTO ANY RESTAURANT IN TOWN AND ORDER ANYTHING I WANT, AND I DON'T HAVE TO GO TO FIFTY-CENT MOVIES ANYMORE, EITHER...I'M JUST SO GREEDY, THE MORE I CAN GET, THE BETTER. MY AMBITION IS TO HAVE A WHOLE BUNCH OF GOLD BULLION. BIG GOLD BARS, I'D LIKE TO HAVE BIG CHUNKS OF GOLD, JUST TO HAVE AROUND THE HOUSE."

JIM MORRISON
THE DOORS

FREDDIE MERCURY
QUEEN

"SPEND IT, MY DEAR. I'M THE ONE MEMBER OF THE BAND FOR WHOM MONEY ISN'T VERY ENDEARING. I'M THE ONE WHO SPENDS IT STRAIGHT OFF. IT JUST GOES. ON CLOTHES, AND I LIKE NICE THINGS AROUND ME."

Melody Maker, December 21, 1974

MONEY (THAT'S WHAT I WANT)

ROBERT PLANT
LED ZEPPELIN

"TO HAVE MONEY AT LAST IS JUST ANOTHER FIGURE IN MY MIND OF MASS ACCEPTANCE WHICH IS WHAT WE ALL WORK FOR. I MEAN EVERYBODY, NO MATTER HOW MUCH THEY WANT TO DENY THE FACT, REALLY WANTS, IN THE END, TO BE ACCEPTED BY THE MAJORITY OF PEOPLE FOR BEING EITHER A TALENT OR A COMMODITY, AND I THINK THAT WE'VE REACHED THAT STAGE NOW."

BBC-TV, *Nationwide*,
September 16, 1970

233

"THE REAL ACTION CAME AT NIGHT, AFTER ALL THE LITTLE BOYS AND GIRLS WERE PUT TO BED, THEIR BELLIES FULL AND THEIR HEADS SPINNING WITH FAIRY TALES. THAT'S WHEN I HIT THE STREETS, DANCING FOR PENNIES AND SHINING SHOES FOR NICKELS, TRYING TO EARN ENOUGH MONEY TO HELP PUT SOME FOOD ON OUR TABLE. EARNING MONEY—NOW THAT *EXCITED* ME. AND BECAUSE I COULD SOMETIMES MAKE AS MUCH AS TEN DOLLARS A DAY, I THOUGHT I HAD LEARNED EVERYTHING I WOULD EVER NEED TO KNOW."

JAMES BROWN

I Feel Good: A Memoir of a Life in Soul,
New American Library, 2005

MONEY (THAT'S WHAT I WANT)

"*BORN TO RUN* HAD EARNED ME A STEINWAY BABY GRAND PIANO AND A 1960 CHEVROLET CORVETTE WITH CRAGAR WHEELS I BOUGHT FOR SIX GRAND FROM A KID BEHIND THE COUNTER AT THE WEST LONG BRANCH CARVEL ICE CREAM STAND."

BRUCE SPRINGSTEEN

Born to Run, Simon & Schuster, 2015

Kerrang!, March 19, 1987

"IT'S THE GREATEST THING, MAN, THAT THREE AVERAGE SHITHEADS LIKE US ARE RIDING AROUND LA IN A WHITE ROLLS ROYCE THE SIZE OF THIS ROOM."

MIKE D
BEASTIE BOYS

MONEY (THAT'S WHAT I WANT)

Smash Hits, May 24-June 6, 1984

"SUDDENLY YOU'RE IN A POSITION WHERE YOU HAVE AS MUCH MONEY AS YOU NEED, YOU FEEL SECURE, AND YOU HAVE NO ONE TO ANSWER TO. IT'S ABSOLUTELY BRILLIANT! WHAT BETTER JOB COULD YOU HAVE THAN THAT?"

GEORGE MICHAEL
WHAM!

FIVE
LEGENDARY RECORDING
Studios

1. GOLD STAR STUDIOS, Los Angeles, CA—Founded in 1950 by Stan Ross and David Gold, this independent studio, in its thirty-four years of operation, hosted many of the most popular and important recording stars of the rock era, including the Beach Boys, Buffalo Springfield, Jimi Hendrix, Neil Young, Sonny & Cher, the Monkees, the Go-Go's, and the Ramones, as well as the highly regarded assemblage of studio musicians known as the "Wrecking Crew." In the sixties, Phil Spector used Gold Star's custom equipment and unique acoustics to create his "wall of sound" with the Ronettes and Righteous Brothers.

2. ELECTRIC LADY STUDIOS, New York, NY—Founded by Jimi Hendrix in 1970 and still in operation today, Electric Lady has recorded many great artists over the years including the Rolling Stones, Stevie Wonder, Patti Smith, David Bowie, the Clash, and AC/DC, as well as Hendrix himself. More

recently, St Vincent, Frank Ocean, Lorde, and Fleet Foxes have all worked in the house that Jimi built.

3. SUN STUDIO, Memphis, Tennessee—The emergence of Rock & Roll in the fifties would be inconceivable without the contribution of Sun Records and its visionary founder Sam Phillips. Originally established as the Memphis Recording Service in 1950, it hosted many of the great R&B artists of the early fifties, including Howlin' Wolf, B.B. King, and Little Walter, but would ultimately cement its legend with Johnny Cash, Jerry Lee Lewis, Carl Perkins, and especially Elvis Presley, who first visited in 1953 to record "My Happiness" for his mother. The King would produce several historic recordings before Phillips sold his contract for a handsome profit to RCA in 1955. Phillips would move to a larger facility in 1959, but the original location on Union Ave was reopened in 1987 as both a museum and working studio. U2, Def Leppard, John Mellencamp, and Beck, among others, have all recorded here since then.

4. ABBEY ROAD STUDIOS, London, England—Established in 1931 by the Gramophone Company, precursor to EMI, in a converted nineteenth century townhouse, it is the oldest continuously operating recording studio in the world, and has recorded many of the greatest artists in music history, beginning with Edward Elgar in 1931. Many other great classical artists would follow, but its emergence as an important Rock

& Roll site begins with the Beatles in 1962. They would produce nearly all of their recorded output here with producer George Martin until 1970. Their final studio album, *Abbey Road*, features a photograph of the Fab Four crossing the road nearby. Many other rock artists have recorded here as well, including Pink Floyd, Amy Winehouse, Blur, Depeche Mode, Michael Jackson, Elton John, Oasis, Queen, and U2.

5. FAME STUDIOS, Muscle Shoals, Alabama—Originally founded by Rick Hall above a drug store in nearby Florence in 1959, FAME (an acronym for Florence Alabama Music Enterprises) produced many great recordings in rock, R&B, pop, and country music over the decades, and continues that legacy today. Early stars included Arthur Alexander, Etta James, the Tams, and Joe Tex. Later in the sixties Atlantic Records producer Jerry Wexler brought Wilson Pickett and Aretha Franklin here to make use of the outstanding session musicians known as the Muscle Shoals Rhythm Section, one of whom was Duane Allman. Many great artists worked here, including Otis Redding, Solomon Burke, Alicia Keys, King Curtis, Tom Jones, George Jones, and Lou Rawls. In 1969 several of the FAME musicians left to create the Muscle Shoals Sound Studio nearby, which has an equally impressive legacy.

chapter nine

FEUDS, RIVALRIES,

and Insults

R ock & Roll's inherent capacity for conflict has provided us with a litany of slurs,
swipes, put-downs, and outright musical
brawls. Songs have been written to throw
rocks, settle scores, and start trouble, often
with hilariously entertaining results.

The Rock & Roll Wisdom Playlist

John Lennon—"How Do You Sleep?"
Lynyrd Skynyrd—"Sweet Home Alabama"
Bob Dylan—"Idiot Wind"
Foo Fighters—"I'll Stick Around"
Mojo Nixon—"Don Henley Must Die"

MORRISSEY

"I WOULD RATHER EAT MY OWN TESTICLES THAN REFORM THE SMITHS. AND THAT'S SAYING SOME-THING FOR A VEGETARIAN."

Uncut, May 2006

FEUDS, RIVALRIES, AND INSULTS

GRAHAM COXON
BLUR

"IT'S LIKE PINK FLOYD. AS A FAN YOU JUST THINK, 'WHAT A BICKERING LOAD OF SELF-OBSESSED OLD LADIES!'"

Mojo, May 2015

"THE WEST COAST WAS TOO FLOWERY FOR WORDS. I MEAN, FLOWER POWER? FUCK OFF. WE HATED THE BANDS. WE HATED THEIR MUSIC. WE HATED THEIR POLITICS. AND WE CERTAINLY HATED THE WAY THEY DRESSED."

JOHN CALE
THE VELVET UNDERGROUND

Uncut, December 2009

FEUDS, RIVALRIES, AND INSULTS

"I DON'T WANT THESE PEOPLE TO TAKE IT PERSONALLY. BUT, I MEAN, JOURNEY STINKS."

DAVID LEE ROTH
VAN HALEN

Creem, October 1981

Creem, October 1981

"I'M GLAD TO SEE THE CLASH HAVE GONE DISCO. IT'S ABOUT TIME THEY MADE SOME MONEY."

DAVID LEE ROTH
VAN HALEN

FEUDS, RIVALRIES, AND INSULTS

Creem, October 1981

"DAVID BYRNE WOULD QUAL- IFY AS AN ARTIST. I MEAN, BY APPEARANCE'S SAKE. HE LOOKS LIKE HE'S DYING."

DAVID LEE ROTH
VAN HALEN

RAY DAVIES
THE KINKS

"I THINK AMERICA'S HAD IT. LOOK AT THE BANDS. GUNS N' ROSES ARE A TOTALLY WIMPY BAND. I HAVE NO RESPECT FOR THEM WHATSOEVER. 'SWEET CHILD O' MINE' IS LIKE A MONKEES SONG, AND YET THEY COME ON WITH THIS ATTITUDE. THEY'RE NOT AS DANGEROUS AS THEY OR THE PUBLIC WANT TO BELIEVE. THEY'RE LIGHT...A POP GROUP. THEY'RE MORE LIKE R.E.M. THAN LED ZEP."

Mojo, June 1994

FEUDS, RIVALRIES, AND INSULTS

JOE STRUMMER
THE CLASH

"I'LL JEER AT HIPPIES BECAUSE THAT'S HELPFUL. THEY'LL REALIZE THEY'RE STUCK IN A RUT AND MAYBE THEY'LL GET OUT OF IT."

Melody Maker, November 13, 1976

"JOE STRUMMER'S NEVER BEEN OVER-ENDOWED WITH WISDOM, HAS HE? I NEVER LIKED THAT BAND. I ALWAYS THOUGHT THEY WERE FAR TOO SERIOUS AND FAR TOO CHILDISH. IT WAS SLOGANEERING. PICK UP A COPY OF KARL MARX, UNDERLINE A FEW SENTENCES AND CALL THAT 'ATTITUDE.' IT'S JUST DAFT."

JOHN
LYDON

Q, June 1994

FEUDS, RIVALRIES, AND INSULTS

"THE ONLY REASON WE GET THAT BAD BOY SHIT IS BECAUSE THE OTHER BANDS IN L.A. ARE SUCH WIMPS."

SLASH
GUNS N' ROSES

Sounds, April 4, 1987

Punk magazine, January 1976

"ISN'T SPRINGSTEEN ALREADY OVER THE HILL? I MEAN, ISN'T EVERYBODY JUST SAYING THAT THEY CONSTRUCTED HIM 'CAUSE THEY NEEDED A ROCK STAR? I MEAN...ALREADY, LIKE GROUPS ARE COMING OUT AND THEY'RE SAYING THEY'RE THE NEW BRUCE SPRINGSTEEN, WHICH IS REALLY... HE WAS ONLY POPULAR FOR A WEEK. WHICH OUGHTA TEACH PEOPLE FROM THE MARINES TO STAY OUTTA MANAGEMENT."

LOU REED

FEUDS, RIVALRIES, AND INSULTS

Spin, January 1986

"I WATCHED THE SO-CALLED LED ZEPPELIN REUNION ON THE AIR AND I'VE NEVER HEARD SUCH A LOT OF FUCKING RUBBISH IN MY LIFE. THAT'S WHAT HAPPENED TO CREAM, AND I DON'T EVER WANT TO GET INTO THAT POSITION AGAIN, WHERE YOU WALK ONSTAGE AND PEOPLE CHEER EVEN IF IT'S FUCKING AWFUL JUST BECAUSE OF WHO YOU ARE."

GINGER BAKER
CREAM

ALBERT HAMMOND, JR.
THE STROKES

"NICK CAVE IS NOT PARTY MUSIC!"

Spin, January 2003

FEUDS, RIVALRIES, AND INSULTS

MICKY DOLENZ
THE MONKEES

"AND TO ALL OF THOSE WHO CRITICIZED, CONDEMNED, BERATED, LAMBASTED, DENOUNCED, DEFAMED, DEFILED, OR OTHERWISE DESECRATED THE MONKEES...GO FUCK YOURSELVES."

I'm a Believer: My Life of Monkees, Music and Madness, Hyperion, 1993

"THAT BLACK EYED PEAS DIRTY DANCING THING IS WORSE THAN RAPING A CAT. WHAT IS WRONG WITH PEOPLE? DO THEY HATE EARS?"

LCD SOUNDSYSTEM

Twitter, March 9, 2011

FEUDS, RIVALRIES, AND INSULTS

"I QUESTION WHAT EMOTION MANILOW TOUCHES. PEOPLE ARE ENTERTAINED BY HIM. BUT ARE THEY EMOTIONALLY MOVED? BY 'MANDY'? BY 'I WRITE THE SONGS'? I DON'T THINK SO. I DON'T BELIEVE ANYTHING THAT BARRY MANILOW SINGS."

PAUL SIMON

Playboy, February 1984

London Calling, January 1995

"[OASIS,] THEY'RE A JOKE AREN'T THEY? IT'S JUST LOTS OF MIDDLE CLASS PEOPLE APPLAUDING A BUNCH OF GUYS WHO ACT STUPID AND WRITE REALLY PRIMITIVE MUSIC AND PEOPLE SAY 'OH IT'S SO HONEST.'"

THOM YORKE
RADIOHEAD

FEUDS, RIVALRIES, AND INSULTS

Esquire UK, November 5, 2015

"I'M AWARE THAT RADIOHEAD HAVE NEVER HAD A FUCKING BAD REVIEW. I RECKON IF THOM YORKE FUCKING SHIT INTO A LIGHT BULB AND STARTED BLOWING IT LIKE AN EMPTY BEER BOTTLE IT'D PROBABLY GET 9 OUT OF 10 IN FUCKING *MOJO*."

NOEL GALLAGHER
OASIS

SIMON LE BON
DURAN DURAN

"I DON'T UNDERSTAND RIVALRY. THERE'S ROOM ENOUGH FOR EVERY-ONE. COMPETITION KEEPS THE BUSINESS HEALTHY AND YOUNG. ALL THE RUBBISH GETS KICKED OUT, AND THAT'S A GOOD THING."

Smash Hits, April 1-14, 1982

FEUDS, RIVALRIES, AND INSULTS

ELTON JOHN

"MADONNA, BEST FUCKING LIVE ACT? FUCK OFF. SINCE WHEN HAS LIP-SYNCING BEEN LIVE? SORRY ABOUT THAT, BUT I THINK EVERYONE WHO LIP-SYNCS IN PUBLIC ONSTAGE WHEN YOU'VE PAID LIKE 75 QUID TO SEE THEM SHOULD BE SHOT. THANK YOU VERY MUCH. THAT'S ME OFF HER FUCKING CHRIST-MAS CARD LIST, BUT DO I GIVE A TOSS? NO."

Q Awards, October 3, 2004

FIVE
NOTORIOUS TELEVISION
Appearances

1. ELVIS PRESLEY ON THE *STEVE ALLEN SHOW* (JULY 1, 1956)—The emerging King of Rock & Roll had been a huge TV hit on NBC for Milton Berle, so the network scheduled him to appear with Steve Allen in New York. Still controversial for his provocative hip-swinging performances, Presley was grudgingly enticed into performing "Hound Dog" in formal attire to a less-than-thrilled basset hound named Sherlock. Elvis's fans were outraged and felt that the host was attempting to publicly humiliate their hero. Presley himself later regretted the appearance and privately vowed never to perform for Allen again.

2. THE DOORS AND THE ROLLING STONES ON THE *ED SULLIVAN SHOW* (1967)—Fresh from securing their first number one with "Light My Fire," the Doors were booked on the *Ed Sullivan Show*, which had been a springboard for many rock acts in the sixties, on September 17, 1967. Not long before air time, a producer alerted Jim Morrison and his bandmates

that they would need to drop the suggestive lyric "higher" in the hit song and replace it with "better." Back on January 15, a similar demand was made of the Rolling Stones, who grudgingly agreed to change the lyrics of "Let's Spend the Night Together" to "Let's Spend Some Time Together." In the resulting performance, Mick Jagger slurred and winked his way through the hit tune, seemingly aware that the audience was in on his apparent charade. It was good enough to satisfy Sullivan, as the Stones would appear on the show again in 1969. Morrison, however, ignored the demand and performed the song unchanged, to the ire of Sullivan and the network. Subsequently, the Doors were not to appear on the show again.

3. ELVIS COSTELLO ON *SATURDAY NIGHT LIVE* (DECEMBER 17, 1977)—Costello and the Attractions were touring the United States in support of his first album, *My Aim Is True*, but were a last-minute replacement for the Sex Pistols, and still relatively unknown to the TV audience. "Watching the Detectives" would be their opening number, but his label, Columbia Records was emphatic that the second be "Less Than Zero," a UK single referencing British fascist Oswald Mosley. Costello reluctantly agreed but felt the tune wouldn't be understood by Americans, so he perpetrated a bait-and-switch by stopping the band only a few seconds in, offered a brief word of apology, and instead blasted "Radio, Radio." Producer Lorne Michaels was not amused, and banned Costello from the show for a dozen years. In 1999, Costello

commemorated the moment in a special anniversary episode of *SNL* by hijacking the Beastie Boys performance of "Sabotage" to again rock "Radio, Radio."

4. FRANKIE LYMON ON *THE BIG BEAT* (JULY 19, 1957)—

Alan Freed was the DJ most responsible for bringing early R&B to white audiences, and even claimed to have invented the term "Rock & Roll." He was also as big a star as many of the performers he featured, and was given his own live television show on ABC, *The Big Beat*, in 1957. The young Frankie Lymon had a huge hit with "Why Do Fools Fall in Love" the previous year and was a huge star, but was shown dancing with a white girl live on national television, to the outrage of ABC's southern affiliates. The network pulled the plug, immediately cancelling the show. *The Big Beat* would return in 1959 as a local New York program, but that wouldn't last either, as Freed was felled by the Payola scandal.

5. SINEAD O'CONNOR ON *SATURDAY NIGHT LIVE* (OCTO-BER 3, 1992)—

Irish singer Sinead O'Connor was well known as a distinctive and powerful performer by 1992, with two successful albums and a hit single "Nothing Compares 2 U." In fact, she had performed on *SNL* the previous year. On October 3, 1992, however, she performed an a cappella rendition of Bob Marley's "War" with some modified lyrics about child abuse. After completing the song she proceeded to tear up a photo of Pope John Paul II directly into the

camera while stating "Fight the real enemy." The studio audience was aghast, and much of the television audience was stunned and outraged. NBC, which had no advance knowledge of what would happen, received over 4,000 calls of complaint. What had been intended as a protest against the abuses of the Catholic church horrified much of the country. Reruns of the show featured the dress rehearsal, which featured no such moment of controversy. O'Connor was pilloried by most of the media. Her career has never fully recovered, but she's remained largely unrepentant.

chapter ten
GENERAL ADVICE
and Observations

When they're not espousing their points of view on all manner of topics in song, rock stars can often be found telling it like they think it is to a reporter. Whether any of it qualifies as advice is a matter of opinion, but even when an observation seems far-fetched, it can still be a lot of fun to hear or read.

The Rock & Roll Wisdom Playlist

Oasis—"Don't Look Back in Anger"
Petula Clark—"Don't Sleep in the Subway"
The Byrds—"Everybody's Been Burned"
R.E.M.—"Everybody Hurts"
Minutemen—"Do You Want New Wave
or Do You Want the Truth?"

"HELL IS OTHER PEOPLE'S PLAYLISTS."

MARK HOPPUS
BLINK 182

Twitter, November 29, 2013

GENERAL ADVICE AND OBSERVATIONS

"EVERYTHING I'VE LEARNED IN LIFE I'VE LEARNED EITHER BY DOING IT OR WATCHING THE CHANGES OTHER PEOPLE GO THROUGH."

CASS ELLIOTT
THE MAMAS AND THE PAPAS

Rolling Stone, October 26, 1968

San Francisco Press Conference, 1965
(as reported in *Rolling Stone* on
January 20, 1968)

"OH, MY HOPES, FOR THE FUTURE: TO BE HONEST, YOU
KNOW, I DON'T HAVE ANY HOPES FOR THE FUTURE
AND I JUST HOPE TO HAVE ENOUGH BOOTS TO BE ABLE
TO CHANGE THEM. THAT'S ALL REALLY, IT DOESN'T
BOIL DOWN TO ANYTHING MORE THAN THAT."

**BOB
DYLAN**

GENERAL ADVICE AND OBSERVATIONS

Rolling Stone, May 28, 1970

"ALL RIGHT EVERYBODY, LET YOUR HAIR DOWN. IF YOU HAVE A WIG TAKE YOUR WIG OFF AND GET DOWN WITH IT. I JUST THINK THAT EVERYBODY NEEDS TO GET DOWN WITH IT, TODAY. ALL THE REAL PEOPLE ARE DOWN WITH IT, BUT IT'S THE SQUARES THAT AIN'T GETTIN' NOWHERE. JUST GET DOWN WITH IT."

LITTLE RICHARD

BONO
U2

"I THINK THE THING I LEAST LIKE ABOUT MYSELF IS THAT I'M REASONABLE. AND BEING REASONABLE IS A VERY UN-POP-STAR TRAIT. SO I AM TAKING BASTARD LESSONS."

Rolling Stone, October 8, 1987

GENERAL ADVICE AND OBSERVATIONS

RINGO STARR
THE BEATLES

"THERE'S 20 MILLION PEOPLE OUT THERE
CAN SING ME OUT OF THE FUCKING ROOM, BUT
THEY'RE NOT GETTING ANYWHERE BECAUSE THEY
CAN ONLY SING. WHATEVER IT IS WITH ME, I
DON'T KNOW. IT'S A KIND, FUN-LOVING ATTITUDE
TO LIFE THAT COMES ACROSS, I THINK. I DON'T
WANT TO HASSLE ANYBODY."

Creem, October 1976

"I MEAN, JUST THE OTHER DAY A GUY SAID TO ME 'HEY MICK, YOU SHOULD REALLY GET YOUR-SELF SOME NICE SHOES AND NOT WEAR THOSE OLD SNEAKERS ALL THE TIME.' I EVEN HAD A SUIT ON AND THIS GUY GOES 'GEE, I THOUGHT YOU'D HAVE BETTER SHOES.' BETTER SHOES!"

MICK JAGGER
THE ROLLING STONES

Creem, January 1978

GENERAL ADVICE AND OBSERVATIONS

"I DON'T PERSONALLY HAVE [A COMPUTER]. A MOUSE, TO ME, I PUT THE CAT ON IT. BUT I HAVE PEOPLE THAT DO, BECAUSE IT'S ABSOLUTELY NECESSARY BECAUSE OF THE SPEED-UP OF COMMUNICATION. THE IDEA OF GOSSIPING ON A TV SCREEN IS, TO ME, VERY BIZARRE, BUT OTHER PEOPLE DO IT QUITE NATURALLY. I'D RATHER LOOK PEOPLE IN THE EYE WHEN I'M TALKING TO THEM. UNLESS IT'S AN IMPORTANT MESSAGE, LIKE 'GET THE HELL OUT OF THERE, THE COPS ARE COMING.'"

KEITH RICHARDS
THE ROLLING STONES

Uncut, December 2002

Record Mirror, November 9, 1968

"WHAT IF EVERYONE WERE TO WALK AROUND NAKED? IT MIGHT BE A BIT COLD, BUT WHAT WOULD BE IMMORAL ABOUT IT?"

MARC BOLAN T-REX

GENERAL ADVICE AND OBSERVATIONS

Q, February 2016

"I ALWAYS FEEL THAT IN A VENUE PEOPLE ARE NICER THAN IN THE STREETS. IT BRINGS THE GOOD OUT. THE PASSION AND THE DESIRE TO FEEL ALIVE, AND TO LOVE, AND TO BE LOVED."

JEHNNY BETH
SAVAGES

RAY DAVIES
THE KINKS

"I WAS IN A LIFT IN NEW YORK CITY AND WANTED TO GO TO THE 50TH FLOOR. A WOMAN CAME IN AND WANTED TO GO TO THE BASEMENT. SHE PRESSED BASEMENT AND I SAID, I WAS IN HERE FIRST, I WANT TO GO TO THE 50TH FLOOR, AND SHE SAID 'SUE ME.' GREAT. I ACCEPTED IT.... A LOT MORE CASUAL, THE AMERICANS."

Rolling Stone, November 26, 1970

GENERAL ADVICE AND OBSERVATIONS

PAUL SIMON

"SOON AS THEY PUT YOU UP THERE AND THEY PUT THE KNIFE IN YOUR BACK, YOU'RE GETTING TO THE BEST PERIOD OF YOUR LIFE. UP UNTIL THAT POINT PEOPLE HAVE BEEN SAYING YOU WERE GREAT, WHEN HALF THE TIME YOU WEREN'T. AND NOW THEY'LL SAY THAT ANYTHING YOU DO IS BAD WHEN IT'S NOT TRUE. THE PRESSURE IS OFF YOU AND THE SPOTLIGHT IS OFF AND YOU CAN PROCEED ALONG WITH YOUR WORK."

Rolling Stone, May 28, 1970

"I USED TO BE REALLY LOUD AND OBNOX-IOUS. AND THEN I STOPPED HANGING OUT WITH PEOPLE."

KURT COBAIN
NIRVANA

Melody Maker, December 19, 1992

GENERAL ADVICE AND OBSERVATIONS

"PRIVATE LIFE? I HAVE NO PRIVATE LIFE. I HAVEN'T READ THE PAPER TODAY SO I DON'T KNOW WHO I'M GOING OUT WITH, WHERE I'M LIVING, WHAT I'M DOING. LET ME READ THE PAPERS FIRST. THEY KNOW MORE THAN ME."

ADAM
ANT

Smash Hits, May 27-June 9, 1982

Smash Hits, March 15-28, 1984

"STUPID HOBBY, REALLY. YOU WAIT FIVE HOURS TO CATCH A FISH, THEN YOU CATCH IT, THEN YOU THROW IT BACK. I REALLY DON'T KNOW WHY I BOTHER."

DAVE GAHAN
DEPECHE MODE

GENERAL ADVICE AND OBSERVATIONS

Smash Hits, May 24-June 6, 1984

"EVERYTHING ABOUT ME IS AVERAGE, EVERYTHING'S NORMAL, IN THE BOOKS. IT'S THE THINGS INSIDE THAT MAKES ME NOT AVERAGE. I'D ALSO CHANGE MY INDECISIVENESS. YES, NO, YES, NO, YES! IN MY BUSINESS CAREER I FEEL I MAKE GOOD DECISIONS, BUT IN MY PERSONAL LIFE I'M CONSTANTLY CREATING HAVOC BY CHANGING MY MIND EVERY FIVE SECONDS."

MADONNA

PRINCE

"THE MOST IMPORTANT THING IS TO BE TRUE TO YOURSELF, BUT I ALSO LIKE DANGER."

Los Angeles Times, November 21, 1982

GENERAL ADVICE AND OBSERVATIONS

BRUCE SPRINGSTEEN

"THE ROCK DEATH CULT IS WELL LOVED AND CHRONICLED IN LITERATURE AND MUSIC, BUT IN PRACTICE, THERE AIN'T MUCH IN IT FOR THE SINGER AND HIS SONG, EXCEPT A GOOD LIFE UNLIVED, LOVERS AND CHILDREN LEFT BEHIND, AND A SIX-FOOT-DEEP HOLE IN THE GROUND. THE EXIT IN A BLAZE OF GLORY IS BULLSHIT."

Born to Run, Simon & Schuster, 2015

"I'M PROBABLY AT MY FITTEST IF I'M DOING TWO HOURS ON STAGE EVERY DAY, HAVING AN ACTIVE SEX LIFE AND EATING WELL."

JOHN TAYLOR
DURAN DURAN

Smash Hits, January 19-February 1, 1984

GENERAL ADVICE AND OBSERVATIONS

"I HAVE A NEW PHILOSOPHY. WHEN I SAY SOMETHING THAT SOUNDS SMART THEN I MEANT IT AND IF I SAY SOMETHING THAT SOUNDS STUPID THEN I DIDN'T."

JOHNNY MARR
THE SMITHS

Twitter, March 18, 2011

"I EXPECT TO HAVE FUN EVERY TIME I LEAVE THE HOUSE. I AM SELDOM LET DOWN."

EDDIE ARGOS
ART BRUT

GENERAL ADVICE AND OBSERVATIONS

Ask Andrew W.K., *The Village Voice*,
July 9, 2014

"GETTING TO SPEND TIME WITH A LOVING DOG IS A TRUE PRIVILEGE."

GEORGE HARRISON
THE BEATLES

"I THINK MUSIC IS THE MAIN INTEREST OF THE YOUNGER PEOPLE. IT DOESN'T REALLY MATTER ABOUT THE OLDER PEOPLE NOW BECAUSE THEY'RE FINISHED ANYWAY. THERE'S STILL GOING TO BE YEARS AND YEARS OF HAVING ALL THESE OLD FOOLS WHO ARE GOVERNING US AND WHO ARE BOMBING US AND DOIN' ALL THAT BECAUSE, YOU KNOW, IT'S ALWAYS THEM. BUT IT'S NO GOOD GETTING HUNG UP ABOUT THEM BECAUSE THE MAIN THING IS TO GET THE KIDS."

Rolling Stone, February 24, 1968

GENERAL ADVICE AND OBSERVATIONS

JOAN JETT

"GIRLS HAVE GOT BALLS. THEY ARE JUST A LITTLE HIGHER UP."

Twitter, November 10, 2013

"I ONLY EAT TWO THINGS FOR LUNCH: BREAKFAST OR SUSHI."

ALBERT HAMMOND, JR.
THE STROKES

Rolling Stone, November 13, 2003

GENERAL ADVICE AND OBSERVATIONS

"SOMEONE ONCE WROTE THAT IN BETWEEN THE LIVES WE LEAD AND THE LIVES WE FANTASIZE ABOUT LIVING IS THE PLACE IN OUR HEADS WHERE MOST OF US ACTUALLY LIVE."

Girl in a Band: A Memoir,
Dey Street Books, 2015

The Talks, *New York Times*, May 11, 2016

"AND I KNOW NOW, FOR SURE, THE PEOPLE THAT ARE MOST IN TOUCH WITH THEIR EMOTIONS AND THEIR FEELINGS, PEOPLE THAT CAN JUST CRY AT THE DROP OF A DIME BECAUSE THEY RELATE SO MUCH TO SOMEONE ELSE'S PAIN OR THEY JUST DON'T CARE HOW THEY LOOK, AND THEY SAY, I'M FEELING THIS WAY TODAY—THOSE ARE THE STRONGEST PEOPLE I KNOW. THOSE ARE THE STRONGEST PEOPLE I KNOW. I THINK YOU ROB YOURSELF OF LIFE, YOU ROB YOURSELF OF YOUR OWN EXPERIENCE WHEN YOU DON'T LET YOURSELF FEEL WHATEVER IT IS THAT YOU FEEL!"

ALICIA KEYS

GENERAL ADVICE AND OBSERVATIONS

Born to Run, Simon & Schuster, 2016

"THE DYNAMIC BETWEEN CREATIVITY AND COMMERCE REMAINS A CONVOLUTED WALTZ. IF YOU WANT TO FLY BY YOUR OWN LIGHTS, REACH THE AUDIENCE YOU FEEL YOUR TALENTS DESERVE AND BUILD A WORK LIFE ON WHAT YOU'VE LEARNED, VALUE AND CAN DO, BE WARY."

BRUCE
SPRINGSTEEN

LEONARD COHEN

"THINK ABOUT THIS SERIOUSLY BEFORE YOU ANSWER: WOULD YOU LIKE A SCOOP OF ICE CREAM IN YOUR COFFEE?"

Mojo, March 2012

GENERAL ADVICE AND OBSERVATIONS

TEN MUST-SEE ROCK DOCUMENTARIES
& Concert Films

1. *T.A.M.I. SHOW* (1964)—A concert film covering two days of late October 1964 shows at the Santa Monica Civic Auditorium, the *T.A.M.I. Show* was released to theaters just two months later. Perfectly capturing the thrill of the rapidly evolving youth culture, the film includes live performances by Marvin Gaye, Smokey Robinson and the Miracles, the Beach Boys, Lesley Gore, Chuck Berry, the Supremes, James Brown and the Famous Flames, and the Rolling Stones.

2. *DON'T LOOK BACK* (1967)—Arriving nearly two years after the 1965 tour of England it covered, *Don't Look Back* gave many Bob Dylan fans a first look at the artist behind the scenes. At times confident and confrontational, even when he's not meant to be the center of attention, Dylan is spellbinding.

3. *WOODSTOCK* (1970)—Legendary documentary showing what many believe is one of the great moments where music and the burgeoning counterculture came together. In addition

to its footage of live performances during the festival, the film also includes conversations with local residents near the Bethel, New York, site, as as well as a look at the crew responsible for cleaning the portable toilets.

4. *GIMME SHELTER* (1970)—Shot during the Rolling Stones' 1969 US tour, *Gimme Shelter* includes footage of the group performing at Madison Square Garden, recording at Muscle Shoals Sound Studio in Alabama, and the chaos that descended upon the increasingly unruly crowd during a free concert at the Altamont Speedway in Tracy, California, which resulted in the stabbing death of concertgoer Meredith Hunter. If Woodstock showed the hippie dream, some critics have posited, *Gimme Shelter* was its nightmare.

5. *WATTSTAX* (1973)—A benefit concert staged at the Los Angeles Memorial Coliseum in August 1972, *Wattstax* was timed to coincide with the seventh anniversary of the Watts Riots. The film stars both the Stax artists who performed, and the thousands upon thousands of fans who paid just a dollar to turn up and dance.

6. *THE LAST WALTZ* (1978)—Director Martin Scorsese's love letter to the Band, *The Last Waltz* documents the group's final show at San Francisco's Winterland Ballroom in November 1976. They were joined onstage by influences and fans alike, such as Bob Dylan, Eric Clapton, Ringo Starr, Muddy Waters, Van Morrison, Joni Mitchell, and Neil Diamond.

7. *STOP MAKING SENSE* (1984)—An electrifying documentation of an elaborately staged run of shows by Talking Heads at Hollywood's Pantages Theater, Jonathan Demme's *Stop Making Sense* succeeds by eschewing live film conventions and focusing instead on the theatricality and sheer power of the group's expanded 1983 lineup. It opens with frontman David Byrne playing "Psycho Killer" on acoustic guitar to a recorded drum machine on a beat box. Song by song the rest of the core members of the band take the stage, and the energy doesn't let up throughout.

8. *DIG!* (2004)—At the core of director Ondi Timoner's debut film is the long, fractious relationship between two groups, the Dandy Warhols and the Brian Jonestown Massacre, whose mercurial ringleader Anton Newcombe is shown as a combustible perfectionist willing to sacrifice everything in following his musical muse. Though members of both bands have dismissed the end result as an oversimplification of a much larger story, it still packs a punch, both dramatically and musically.

9. *SHUT UP AND PLAY THE HITS* (2012)—That LCD Soundsystem went on to reunite five years after their very public end, the documentary covering their funereal party at Madison Square Garden in April 2011 is no less riveting. Intercut with live footage from that "final" show are surprisingly tender, emotional moments with its members as they contemplate what they mean to one another, and what it means to move on.

10. ***THIS IS SPINAL TAP*** (1984)—More a "mockumentary" than documentary, *This is Spinal Tap* apparently so often hit the mark on the excess of life in a Rock & Roll band that it felt uncomfortably real for many actual rock stars. Filmed in documentary style by Rob Reiner, the movie follows the fictional heavy metal band Spinal Tap during a tour of America, with plenty of awkward and hilarious moments both on and off stage, and actual music performed by the film's stars that goes to 11.